THE
AMAZING
DISCOVERIES OF
100 BRILLIANT
SCIENTISTS

THE
AMAZING
DISCOVERIES OF
100 BRILLIANT
SCIENTISTS

Abigail Wheatley,
Lan Cook & Rob Lloyd Jones

Illustrated by Léonard Dupond
& Roxane Campoy

Edited by Ruth Brocklehurst
Designed by Samuel Gorham,
Lenka Hrehova & Alice Reese
Managing Designer: Stephen Moncrieff

Consultant: Dr. Mike Kearney

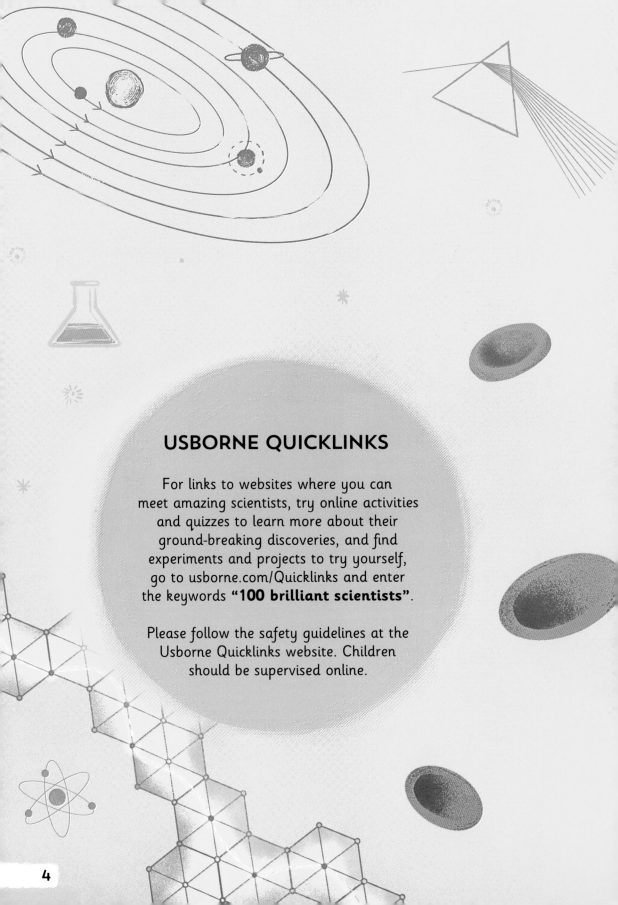

USBORNE QUICKLINKS

For links to websites where you can meet amazing scientists, try online activities and quizzes to learn more about their ground-breaking discoveries, and find experiments and projects to try yourself, go to usborne.com/Quicklinks and enter the keywords **"100 brilliant scientists"**.

Please follow the safety guidelines at the Usborne Quicklinks website. Children should be supervised online.

WHAT MAKES A SCIENTIST BRILLIANT?

Anyone can be a scientist, from a physics professor gazing at distant galaxies to a child watching a caterpillar on a leaf. But only a few scientists have dreamed up mind-blowing theories or made earth-shattering discoveries.

Some scientists have found fame, or won awards such as the Nobel Prizes in chemistry, physics and medicine, which recognize the highest achievements in those areas. But, throughout history, many scientists – all too often women and those from non-western backgrounds – were overlooked, until recent times.

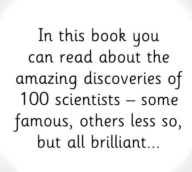

In this book you can read about the amazing discoveries of 100 scientists – some famous, others less so, but all brilliant...

THE MOST AMAZING COMPUTER
THAT NEVER WAS

In the 1830s, when the most complex machines around were engines powered by steam, British mathematician **Charles Babbage** designed what would have been the first true **computer** – if only he'd had the money to build it.

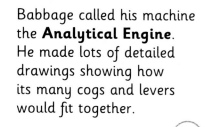

Babbage called his machine the **Analytical Engine**. He made lots of detailed drawings showing how its many cogs and levers would fit together.

BABBAGE'S PLAN

Numbers and instructions would be input using **cards** with holes punched in them. These cards would press various **levers**, which would activate brass **cogs** and **gears** to make calculations.

Modern scientists who have studied Babbage's plans calculate that his machine would have **worked perfectly**.

Babbage designed his computer with a **memory** capable of storing very large numbers – up to 50 decimal points.

THE FIRST EVER
COMPUTER
PROGRAMMER

Ada Lovelace, also a British mathematician, met Babbage and became fascinated by his design.

The Analytical Engine... can do whatever we know how to order it to perform.

Lovelace saw immediately just how powerful such a machine could be. She wrote instructions to tell the Analytical Engine how to make a particular type of **calculation**. This was the world's first **computer program**.

Lovelace's program was what's now known as an **algorithm** – a set of instructions. Today, algorithms are the basis of all computer programs.

UNEARTHING EVIDENCE OF
WHAT KILLED THE DINOSAURS

There have been many theories over the years about what caused **dinosaurs** to die out. In 1980 a father and son team put forward an idea that is now widely accepted as the most likely cause of the dinosaurs' sudden **extinction**.

ITALY, 1977

While studying rock formations, American geologist **Walter Alvarez** became fascinated with **three distinct layers** he found in the rock.

The **top** layer contained fossils of a single **prehistoric** species of foraminifera – a tiny marine creature...

...below that, he could see a peculiar layer of dark, hardened **clay**...

...while the **bottom** layer had many **dinosaur fossils** in it.

The bottom layer, which contained the dinosaur remains, must have formed when dinosaurs were still **alive**. By the time the top layer had formed, with no dinosaur fossils in it, the dinosaurs had **died out**.

Walter realized the dark clay could hold a **clue**. He decided to talk to his father **Luis**, a Nobel Prize winning physicist, about it.

BACK IN AMERICA...

Luis suggested they test the clay layer. The tests showed a surprising amount of an element called **iridium**. Iridium is incredibly rare on Earth, and most of it only arrives when **meteorites** come crashing down from **space**.

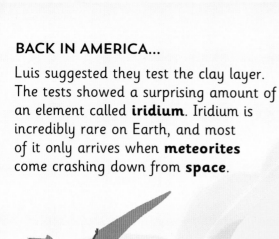

Gradually, Walter and Luis pieced together an account of what must have happened. An enormous meteorite had hit Earth. Its **impact** blasted huge amounts of rock and dust into the air.

They theorized that rocky debris had fallen back to Earth, creating a **fire storm**. Dust hung in Earth's atmosphere for months, possibly years. It **blocked out** the Sun, killing most plants. With nothing to eat, all the dinosaurs and many other animals died out. The dust eventually settled to form the dark layer of hard clay Walter had been studying.

In 1991, scientists identified the vast **Chicxulub crater** on the Yucatan Peninsula, in Mexico, as the most likely impact site of the meteorite that killed off the dinosaurs.

THINKING A WAY THROUGH
BLACK HOLES

Around 1915, scientists started thinking about **black holes** – mysterious areas with such strong gravity that not even light can escape from inside them. Fifty years later, **Stephen Hawking**, a British physicist, set about finding out how black holes work.

1962, STARTING OUT...

When Hawking started working on black holes, they were just a theory. Then, two years later, physicist Roger Penrose made a breakthrough, proposing that black holes can **form** when a dying star collapses in on itself.

GROWING...

In 1972, Hawking suggested that black holes can **grow** by merging, but can't shrink.

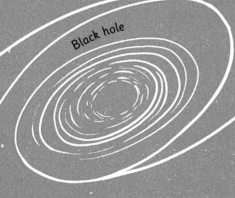

Black hole

...AND SHRINKING

But in 1974, he realized that black holes can **shrink** when they spit out particles. These particles are now known as **Hawking radiation**.

Two black holes merging

Hawking radiation

In 2016, scientists detected disturbances caused by two black holes as they joined together. This was the first **direct proof** that black holes really do exist.

FINDING THE FORMULA
BEHIND ELECTRONS AND ANTI-ELECTRONS

Almost everything in the Universe is made from tiny particles called **atoms**. But there are even smaller particles, including **electrons**. By the 1920s, scientists knew that electrons could exist inside or outside atoms, but weren't sure exactly how they behaved. Enter physicist **Paul Dirac**...

Electron

BRITAIN, 1925

Dirac wrote a new mathematical **formula** to describe how electrons moved **inside atoms**. But there was still no formula to describe how electrons moved **outside atoms**.

TWO YEARS LATER...

Dirac solved this problem with another formula — the **Dirac Equation**. But it had an unexpected twist. It seemed to suggest there were twice as many electrons in the Universe as Dirac had expected.

He realized that each **electron** must have an opposite, **anti-electron**, and that, if the two met, they would **cancel** each other out in a flash of **energy**.

Positron

AMERICA, 1932

...the first anti-electron, or **positron**, was officially detected. Since then, many different anti-particles have been discovered. Together, they're called **antimatter**. Dirac's brilliant equation is now the basis of **quantum field theory**, which is used to study the tiniest particles.

11

SOLVING THE BIGGEST (AND SMALLEST)
PROBLEMS IN THE UNIVERSE

By the 1890s, many scientists thought pretty much everything in **physics** had already been discovered. But then a scientific genius thought up idea after **mind-blowing** new idea. His theories – most of them published in just one year – paved the way for new technology that **changed the world**.

German-American physicist **Albert Einstein** noticed that the laws of physics, such as Newton's idea of **gravity**, didn't always work exactly for **tiny things** such as beams of light, or **vast things** such as stars and planets.

IN 1905...

Einstein showed that, although **light** behaves like **waves**, it's made from tiny **particles**, or **photons**. This won him a **Nobel Prize**.

This work also created a new area called **quantum physics**, studying the tiniest particles. And this led to **inventions** that use these particles, such as **computers** and **lasers**.

ALSO IN 1905...

Einstein theorized that **light** beaming across space had a **fixed** speed, while **space** and **time** had **different** dimensions – depending where you measured them from.

This theory, **Special Relativity** or **SR**, led to the idea of **spacetime** – joining three dimensions of space (**height**, **width** and **depth**) with a fourth, **time**.

STILL IN 1905...

Einstein realized that **energy** could be converted to **mass**. He wrote this as an equation –

$$E=mc^2$$

This proved that particles such as **atoms** had vast amounts of **energy inside them**. This led to the development of **nuclear power** and **bombs**.

LATER...

Einstein combined SR with **gravity**. He saw that gravity from massive things such as planets **bent** spacetime. He called this theory **General Relativity**, or **GR**.

Experiments show that GR is the **best explanation yet** of how the Universe works. But, to Einstein's lifelong regret, GR **can't explain** how the **smallest particles** behave.

HOW A MATHEMATICIAN CREATED
ZERO OUT OF NOTHING

In ancient times, there was no way of writing down **zero**. Most mathematicians simply left a **space**. But this could be confusing because 1 could mean 1, 10 or 100 depending on the size of the space. One mathematician ended this confusion...

INDIA, THE YEAR 628

An astronomer and mathematician named **Brahmagupta** was the first to write a book that set out **mathematical rules** for using zero. It also dealt with numbers smaller than zero, known as **negative numbers**.

Like most Indian mathematicians at the time, I wrote my book entirely in **verse**, to help others memorize my ideas.

Later, Brahmagupta's book was **translated** into Arabic and studied by the mathematician Al-Khwarizmi, whose writings spread to Europe. From there, the concept of zero eventually spread throughout the world.

THE HUMAN ALGORITHM
WHO CHANGED THE FACE OF NUMBERS

Just one mathematician was responsible for popularizing the way of **writing numbers** that we use today. Two new words were also invented because of him: **algebra** – a type of mathematics he invented – and **algorithm**. He lived 12 centuries ago in what is now Afghanistan, and his name was **Muhammad ibn Musa al-Khwarizmi**.

THE COMPENDIOUS BOOK

Around the year 820, Al-Khwarizmi wrote a book called *The Compendious Book on Calculation by Completion and Balancing*, or in **Arabic** *Al-kitab al-mukhtasar fi hisab al-gabr wa'l-muqabala*.

In it he set out a type of calculation that became known as **algebra** – after the Arabic word *al-gabr* (meaning **completion** or **rejoining of broken parts**) in the book's title.

Al-Khwarizmi based some of his work on earlier **Indian** mathematics, adopting the **Hindu** way of writing numbers. Later, his books were translated, spreading this number system (with a few changes) to **Europe** and, eventually, across the **world**.

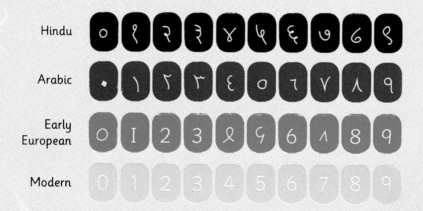

Hindu

Arabic

Early European

Modern

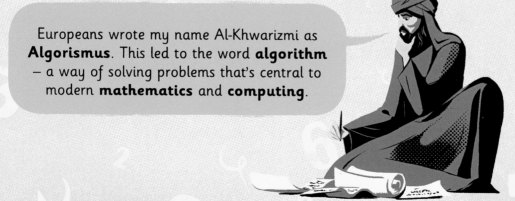

Europeans wrote my name Al-Khwarizmi as **Algorismus**. This led to the word **algorithm** – a way of solving problems that's central to modern **mathematics** and **computing**.

HOW SKY-HIGH AMBITIONS
POWERED THE FIRST FLIGHT

Before 1903, no one had ever managed to fly and control an **engine-powered aircraft**. Two brothers from Ohio, in the United States, were determined to change that...

The brothers, **Orville and Wilbur Wright**, ran a business building bicycles. But their real passion was **flight**. Other inventors had built aircraft with engines, but they were too heavy to fly and there was no way to control them even if they could get into the air.

FROM GLIDERS TO PLANES

In 1902, the brothers tested an uncrewed **glider** for over 700 flights, gathering ideas for a new **flying machine**.

A year later, they designed the **Wright Flyer** — an aircraft with wings that twisted slightly to control its flight, and a **lightweight engine** to power a **propeller**.

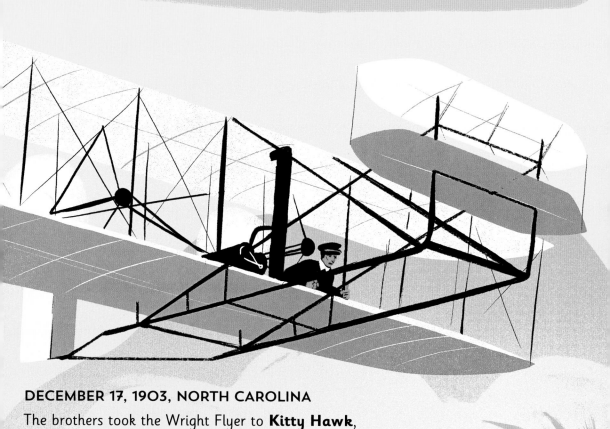

DECEMBER 17, 1903, NORTH CAROLINA

The brothers took the Wright Flyer to **Kitty Hawk**, a town in North Carolina, with steady wind and sand for soft landings. Orville flew it for 12 seconds, around 37m (120ft) – the **first ever** piloted and powered flight!

Over the next few years, the brothers improved their plane design. Soon they could fly for over half an hour, until the engine ran out of fuel. It was the start of the age of engine-powered flight.

LEARNING HOW TO USE
ELECTRICITY

In the early 1800s, several scientists began to experiment with electricity. Physicist **Michael Faraday** understood this mysterious force better than any other...

In his laboratory in London, Faraday made radical discoveries about how **electricity** and **magnetism** are linked, and how to put these incredible forces to use.

In one experiment, Faraday rotated a coil of wire between the two ends (poles) of a U-shaped magnet. He showed that moving a wire through a **magnetic field produced** electricity.

In another, Faraday dipped a wire and a magnet into mercury, a metal that's liquid at room temperature. When he passed electricity along the wire, it started spinning. This was the **first electric motor**.

Then Faraday turned a copper disc between the poles of a magnet to create an electric current. This was the **first electric generator**.

Faraday's discoveries showed that electricity could be used to **power machines**. His influential work paved the way for many modern technologies.

DISCOVERING THE
SECRETS OF FIRE

Until the late 1700s, no one really understood **combustion** — how and why things burn. One scientist discovered the reason, and named **new chemical elements** in the process.

BEFORE 1772...

...most scientists believed fire was caused by an **unknown element** that disappeared during **combustion**.

French chemist **Antoine Lavoisier** wasn't convinced. He found that when he burned certain substances in air, what was left behind became **acidic**.

Lavoisier suspected the substances had **combined** with something **in the air** that was vital for combustion. He called it **oxygen**, which means "acid generator" in Greek.

Lavoisier burned substances in sealed jars, weighing them before and after. The **mass** of the substance burned was the **same** as the substances created. So **nothing had been lost**.

From this, Lavoisier formed the **Law of Conservation of Mass** — still one of the most important rules in science.

IN 1789...

Lavoisier wrote the **first chemistry textbook**. It described all the elements he'd discovered — 33 in total — and suggested a system of **naming** chemicals that scientists still use today.

BRILLIANT NEW IDEAS ABOUT
ELECTRICITY AND MAGNETISM

Many technologies that we take for granted today exist
thanks to the discoveries of one brilliant physicist...

In 1873, British physicist **James Clerk Maxwell** published four equations – known as **Maxwell's Laws** – that describe how **electricity** and **magnetism** interact with each other.

Maxwell showed that they are parts of the **same force**, which travels as **waves**, now called **electromagnetic radiation**. Maxwell realized that **light** is a form of electromagnetic radiation. Later scientists discovered other kinds, too.

The full range of this radiation, shown here, is known as the **electromagnetic spectrum**.

Gamma rays (each wave is shorter than the width of an atom)

X-rays (these waves can pass through some substances, but not others)

Ultraviolet light (we can't see this light but it can harm us)

The **light we can see** (red has the longest and violet has the shortest wavelengths)

Infra red radiation (given off by hot objects)

Microwaves (long electromagnetic waves)

Radio waves (very long waves we use to carry signals and messages)

My discoveries led to the invention of technologies that rely on electromagnetic waves, such as radio, television, satellites and smartphones.

HOW A SNOWY WALK
MADE TRACKS FOR A NOBEL PRIZE

In the 1930s, rival scientists raced to find out how to
split atoms – the tiny building blocks from which almost
everything is made – in order to **release energy** from inside them.
One physicist played a vital part, when others were baffled...

GERMANY, 1938

Physics professor **Lise Meitner**
was studying **radioactivity**
with a colleague, Otto Hahn. But
Meitner had to flee to Sweden
because her family was Jewish –
the German leader, Adolf Hitler,
was **persecuting Jews**.

SWEDEN, THAT WINTER...

Meitner had a **letter** from Hahn
asking for help. He had **bombarded**
a heavy radioactive element,
uranium, with tiny particles. This had
produced a light radioactive element,
barium, but Hahn didn't know why.

During a snowy walk with another physicist,
Otto Frisch, Meitner reasoned that a heavy
uranium atom must have **split** in two,
producing lighter elements, including **barium**.
She and Frisch published this idea one day
after Hahn published his results.

Hahn later received a **Nobel Prize** for his
work on splitting atoms. Experts now agree
Meitner should have been included too.

FINDING A NEW PLANET
THAT WAS NEARLY NAMED GEORGE

Since ancient times, star-gazers and **astronomers** had looked up from the Earth and seen five large objects that moved across the night sky. The ancient Greeks called them **planets**, and the Romans named them Mercury, Venus, Mars, Jupiter and Saturn. No one dreamed there were any more, until an astronomer with a telescope spotted another...

BRITAIN, 1774

William Herschel, a German-born musician, became interested in **astronomy** and learned how to build his own **telescopes**. He spent hours in his garden peering at the night sky.

SEVEN YEARS LATER...

In 1781, while looking at some stars, William noticed something faint and round. When he discussed it with other astronomers, they agreed it must be an **unknown planet**.

PLANET GEORGE?

William wanted to name the planet after Britain's king, **George III**, but astronomers decided on the name **Uranus**. Even so, King George was so pleased with William that he gave him the title **King's Astronomer**.

During his lifetime, William Herschel identified **thousands** of other new objects in the night sky, including **moons** around the planets Saturn and Uranus.

HOW A COMET
PAID A SCIENTIST'S SALARY

Caroline Herschel started her career in astronomy as an assistant to her famous brother William, but before long she made her own **discoveries**. One of them was a **comet** – a dusty, icy lump hurtling through space. This was so impressive that two kings gave her awards.

STARTING OUT

At first, Caroline just assisted William with skilled tasks such as **polishing mirrors** for telescopes, and taking **detailed notes** of what he saw in the sky.

INDEPENDENCE

Then, in 1783, William built Caroline her own telescope, enabling her to explore the skies **for herself**.

A BIG DISCOVERY

In 1786, Caroline spotted a glowing object moving across the sky. It was a **comet**. She was the first to observe it, and it was named **Comet C/1786 P1 (Herschel)**. She became famous overnight.

A year later, the British king, **George III**, granted her a salary, making her the first **paid woman scientist** in Britain. She went on to discover more comets, gas clouds and star clusters. In 1846 King **Frederick William IV** of Prussia (now part of Germany) gave her a gold medal for science.

DISCOVERING WHERE TO FIND
ELECTRONS INSIDE ATOMS

In 1897, British Physicist J.J. Thomson discovered minute particles called **electrons** inside **atoms**. Until then, scientists had thought that atoms were the smallest particles. Thomson suggested electrons were spread throughout the atom, but other scientists came up with different diagrams of atoms (known as **models**) to show where electrons can be found inside an atom.

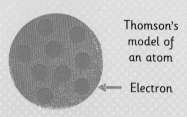

Thomson's model of an atom

← Electron

BRITAIN, 1909-1911

New Zealand physicist **Ernest Rutherford** fired tiny particles at atoms. He caculated that, if Thomson's model was right, the particles would **pass through** the atoms. In fact, quite a few of the particles **bounced off**, as if they had hit something solid inside the atoms.

Rutherford's model of an atom

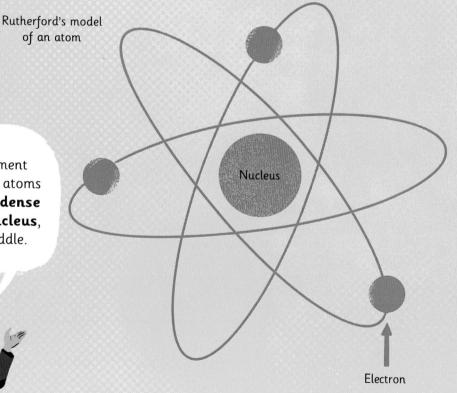

Nucleus

My experiment showed that atoms have a very **dense** clump, or **nucleus**, in their middle.

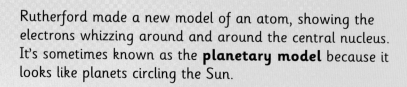

Electron

Rutherford made a new model of an atom, showing the electrons whizzing around and around the central nucleus. It's sometimes known as the **planetary model** because it looks like planets circling the Sun.

ANOTHER RETHINK...

In 1912, Danish physicist **Niels Bohr** argued that, if electrons whizzed around as Rutherford suggested, they would **lose energy** and fall into the nucleus, making the atom **collapse**.

So, Bohr put forward a different model of the atom, with electrons **circling** at certain fixed distances – or **orbits** – around the nucleus.

Bohr also suggested that electrons could **jump** between orbits, losing or gaining set amounts – or **quanta** – of energy.

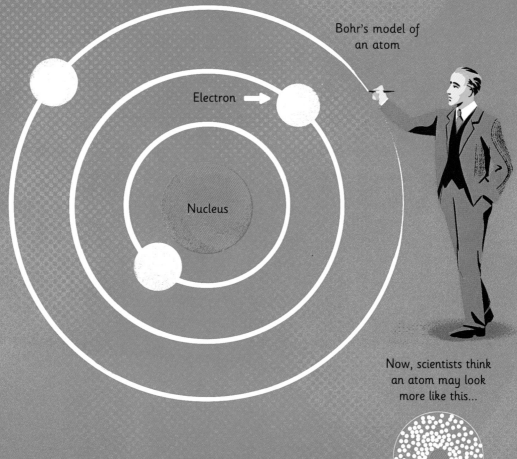

Bohr's model of an atom

Electron

Nucleus

Now, scientists think an atom may look more like this...

These aren't electrons, but the many possible positions of electrons.

A QUANTUM LEAP...

Bohr's idea tied in with the ideas of Einstein (see page 12) and other scientists, and helped create **quantum physics**, a new way of studying the very tiniest particles.

OR TWO...

Later research suggests electrons in atoms don't behave as predictably as Bohr thought. This means it's harder to pin down exactly where in an atom they are.

FINDING A NEW VIEW
OF THE UNIVERSE

The first **telescope** was invented in 1608. It immediately revolutionized astronomy, enabling astronomers to see further into space, and in more detail. One of the first pioneers of this new invention was the Italian astronomer and physicist **Galileo Galilei**.

A YEAR OF DISCOVERIES, 1609-1610

Galileo began to develop and use his own telescopes. This enabled him see **craters** and **mountains** on the **Moon**. Until then, people had believed the Moon was a perfectly smooth, translucent sphere.

The Moon

Galieo discovered **four moons** orbiting **Jupiter**. He also observed that **Venus** went through phases just like the Moon.

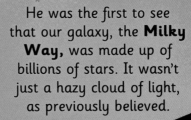

He was the first to see that our galaxy, the **Milky Way,** was made up of billions of stars. It wasn't just a hazy cloud of light, as previously believed.

Jupiter and moons

Phases of Venus

Galileo's observations helped to prove that the planets orbit the **Sun**. At the time, the accepted idea was that everything in the Universe went around the **Earth**.

His ideas were seen as such a threat to authority that in 1633 he was put on trial, and spent the rest of his life under house arrest.

THE FOSSIL EXPERT WHO DISCOVERED
EXTINCTION

Until the late 1700s, if scientists came across bones that didn't belong to any type of animal they recognized, they assumed the animal came from an unexplored part of the world. But, French zoologist, **Georges Cuvier**, came up with a new theory...

CURIOUS BONES

In 1796, Cuvier became fascinated by some **ancient fossilized bones** kept at the National Museum of Natural History in Paris.

While **similar** to elephant bones, they had **crucial differences**. He searched for an animal that **matched** the bones, but couldn't find one.

The bones must belong to a type of elephant-like creature that's **died out**!

It was clear, he argued, that it is possible for an entire species to become **extinct**, or die out. Remains such as the ichthyosaur found by Mary Anning (see page 48) later supported his idea.

Cuvier went on to form the theory that huge reptiles – **dinosaurs** – had once dominated the Earth. But, like the animal whose bones he first studied in Paris, they too had become extinct.

DISCOVERING THE
SECRET OF LIFE

In 1869, a mysterious substance called **DNA** was discovered inside cells – the tiny building blocks that make up living things.
By the 1950s, scientists realized that DNA was what enabled cells to **copy themselves**, but they didn't know how. If they could find out the **shape** of DNA, the answer might become clear...

THE X FACTOR

In 1952, British chemist **Rosalind Franklin** took X-ray photos of microscopic DNA crystals.

Even this cutting-edge method couldn't show exactly what DNA looked like, but it gave some clues. Franklin's clearest **photo** showed smudgy lines arranged in an **X-shape**.

Franklin suspected this meant DNA had a **twin spiral** structure, but she wanted to take time to make sure.

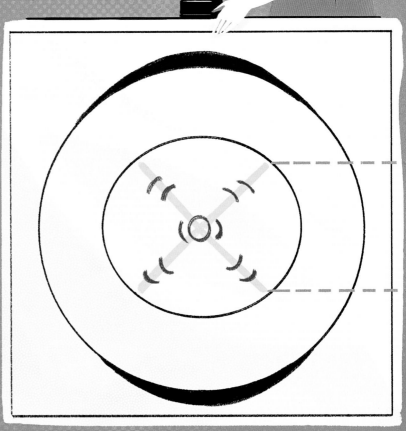

Franklin's photo looked like this. The X-shape was made by the X-ray. The smudgy lines (in brownish red) are where the X-rays cut across a DNA crystal. Follow the dotted lines across to see how they map onto DNA's twin spiral shape...

A RIVAL TEAM

Biologists **James Watson** and **Francis Crick** were already studying the structure of DNA in another part of Britain when they saw Franklin's X-ray photo. This convinced them that DNA really was a twin spiral shape. They gave this shape the name **double helix**.

They realized that, when a cell starts to copy itself, the two spirals of the double helix **unzip**. Each spiral then builds itself up into a **new** double helix, making **two sets** of DNA. The cell **splits** into two new cells, each with its own set of DNA. Each of these new cells is the start of a new living thing.

GRABBING HEADLINES

In 1953, Crick and Watson published their ideas, claiming they had discovered the secret of life. Later, they received a **Nobel Prize**, but Franklin was not included. Many feel that her crucial work was not properly recognized.

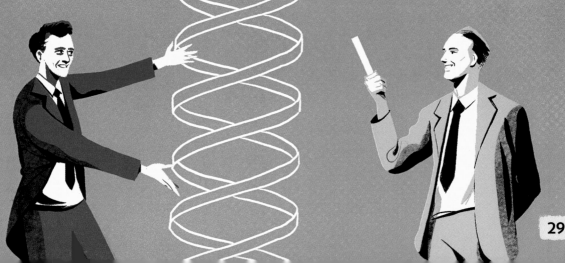

THE SCIENCE OF GENETICS
GREW FROM STUDYING PEA PLANTS

Parents pass on certain **traits** to their children, such as red hair or long legs. No one knew how this worked until a Czech monk named **Gregor Mendel** found the answer – by studying **pea plants**.

A SIMPLE EXPERIMENT

In 1856, Mendel took one pea plant with **green** peas and one with **yellow** peas. Then he bred them together to see what would happen.

To his surprise...

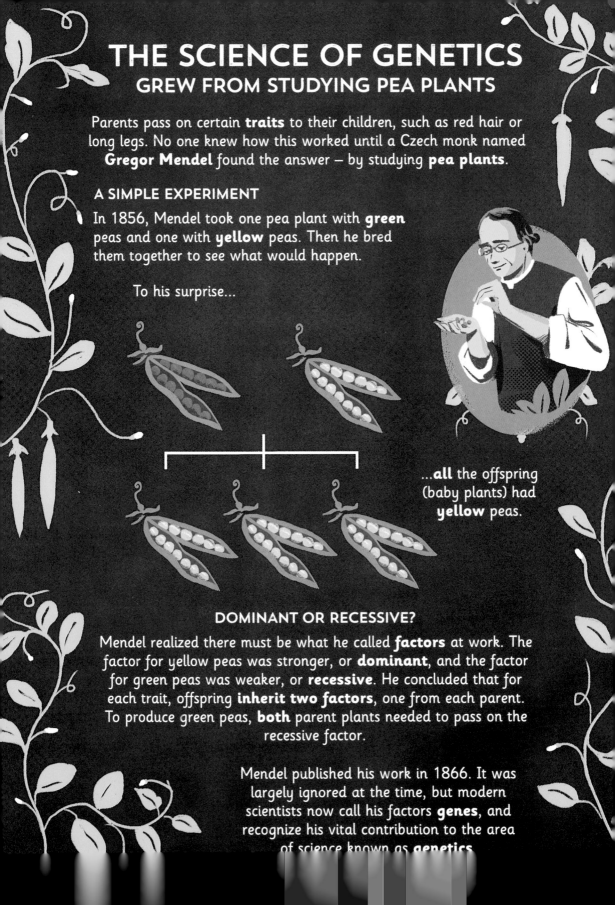

...**all** the offspring (baby plants) had **yellow** peas.

DOMINANT OR RECESSIVE?

Mendel realized there must be what he called **factors** at work. The factor for yellow peas was stronger, or **dominant**, and the factor for green peas was weaker, or **recessive**. He concluded that for each trait, offspring **inherit two factors**, one from each parent. To produce green peas, **both** parent plants needed to pass on the recessive factor.

Mendel published his work in 1866. It was largely ignored at the time, but modern scientists now call his factors **genes**, and recognize his vital contribution to the area of science known as **genetics**.

HOW CORN PLANTS SHOWED THAT
GENES CAN JUMP

In the 1920s, the science of **genetics** was still fairly new and there was much to be discovered. One American geneticist gave scientists a better understanding of how genes work, through her groundbreaking study of **corn** (maize) **genes**.

AMERICA, 1920s–1950s

While researching corn genes, geneticist **Barbara McClintock** became fascinated by different shades of kernels growing on the **same** cob.

She discovered that kernels of different shades all contained the **same** genes, but arranged in a **different order**. She realized the order was what created the different shades.

McClintock planted hundreds of corn plants and carefully studied their **genes**.

Genes from a yellow kernel

Genes from a red kernel

JUMPING GENES

Genes are arranged in strings. McClintock found that genes can **jump around** within these strings, turning certain traits **on** or **off**.

This discovery excited McClintock, but it took 30 years for her work to be acknowledged. In 1983 she was awarded a **Nobel Prize**.

HOW SOME SMALL BIRDS
CHANGED THE HISTORY OF SCIENCE

Over the centuries, many scientists have looked at the amazing **variety** of **living things**, and tried to discover why some are so similar and some are so different. British naturalist **Charles Darwin** spent most of his life coming up with an answer – helped by some small birds called finches.

VOYAGE OF DISCOVERY

In 1831, aged 22, Darwin set sail on a long **voyage around the world**, observing thousands of plants and animals along the way.

Stopping at the Galápagos Islands in the Pacific Ocean, Darwin noticed many **different types** of **finches** spread across the islands.

Some of the finches had **different beak shapes**, and **ate different foods**. Darwin wondered how these differences had come about.

Eats leaves

Eats insects

Eats grubs

Eats seeds

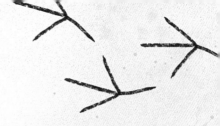

FROM FINCHES TO PIGEONS

In 1836, Darwin returned to Britain. Later, he started breeding **pigeons**. He noticed that differences were **passed** from parent pigeons to their young, and that sometimes these differences even became **exaggerated**.

For example, two **sharp-beaked** pigeons could produce an even **sharper-beaked** baby. Darwin realized a similar process was happening in the wild, and the Galápagos finches were just one example.

FROM PIGEONS TO FINCHES

In the wild, a sharp beak might help a finch pick up insects. That finch would get **more food** than its blunt-beaked siblings, and find it easier to **survive**. Darwin called this idea **natural selection**.

Two sharp-beaked finches might have sharper-beaked babies. Those would be more likely to survive and have babies too. So, sharp beaks would become **more common**, until all insect-eating finches had them. Darwin called this idea **evolution**.

Sharp-beaked parent

Sharp-beaked parent

Even sharper- beaked offspring

GIVE IT TIME

Darwin realized this meant that, after many small changes over a long time, **one type** (or species) of creature could **change** into **another type** (or species) of creature.

In 1859, Darwin published his ideas in a book – **_On the Origin of Species_**. There was an outcry from people who thought Darwin's ideas went against the teachings of the Bible. Some still disagree with **evolution by natural selection**, but for most scientists this idea is the **key** to understanding the natural world.

THE SCIENTIST WHOSE NAME
EXPLODED INTO FAME

Just a handful of scientists have had a particle named after them, but only one lived to see that particle detected. He is British physicist **Peter Higgs**, and his particle was found using a huge machine called the **Large Hadron Collider**, or LHC.

Large Hadron Collider
Path of particles

In the 1950s, physicists studying the tiniest particles theorized there were two types: **fermions** named after Enrico Fermi (see page 56) and **bosons** named after Satyendra Nath Bose — see page 54.

In 1964, Higgs was one of six scientists to **predict** a new type of boson, called the **Higgs boson**.

In 2010, a group of physicists based in Switzerland began using the LHC — a machine for detecting minute particles.

The LHC sends particles along looping tubes, making them go **faster and faster**...

...until they **collide** together, creating other particles such as bosons.

In **2012**, the LHC recorded traces of a Higgs boson. This was the first **scientific evidence** for the Higgs boson, and I became famous.

THE SCIENTIST WHO INVENTED
THE WORLD WIDE WEB

In 1982, the **internet** already existed, but it wasn't big, it wasn't easy to use and it wasn't for everyone. One scientist changed all that by **inventing the World Wide Web**...

SMALL BEGINNINGS

The early internet was a **small network** of computers that shared information between a few American **IT specialists** in universities and businesses.

Users had to switch between **computers** or **programs** to see different pieces of information.

BRANCHING OUT

In 1989, **Tim Berners-Lee,** a British IT expert, adapted existing technology such as **hypertext** (clickable links) to help computers to **share** information more easily.

Then, in 1991 Berners-Lee wrote the first **web pages** and **web browser** – a program to access web pages. The **World Wide Web** was born.

Today, the **Web** has **good and bad** sides – from social media and entertainment to cyber crime and bullying. There are many problems still to solve, but it's impossible to imagine life without it.

THE SCIENTIST WHO
LOOKED A FLEA IN THE EYE

Microscopes are instruments used to view objects too small to be seen with the naked eye. They have been essential to scientific research for hundreds of years. Thought to have been invented around **1590**, they opened up an astonishing new world to scientists.

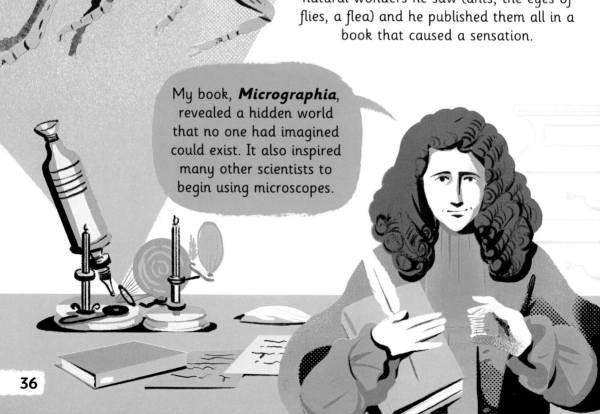

ENGLAND, 1660s

A scientist named **Robert Hooke** designed his own improved microscope. It had a focusing knob and a lens that reflected more light onto what he was looking at.

Tiny details were magnified. Looking at tree bark, Hooke noticed it was made up of rows of tiny rectangular structures, like rooms in a building. He called them **cells** after the word for small rooms in Latin.

Hooke made **detailed drawings** of the natural wonders he saw (ants, the eyes of flies, a flea) and he published them all in a book that caused a sensation.

My book, *Micrographia*, revealed a hidden world that no one had imagined could exist. It also inspired many other scientists to begin using microscopes.

MYSTERIOUS RAYS
THAT MADE THE INVISIBLE VISIBLE

Until the late 19th century, the only way for doctors to see what was happening inside a patient's body was to open it up. Then, in 1895, German physicist **Wilhem Röntgen** made an accidental discovery that revolutionized medical science...

IN A DARK LAB...

Röntgen was experimenting to see what happened when he passed electricity through a glass tube covered with black paper. Suddenly, he noticed a **glow** on the other side of the room. It was coming from a small screen coated with **chemicals**.

He realized that the glow was caused by **rays** coming through the glass tube, **reacting** with the chemicals on the screen.

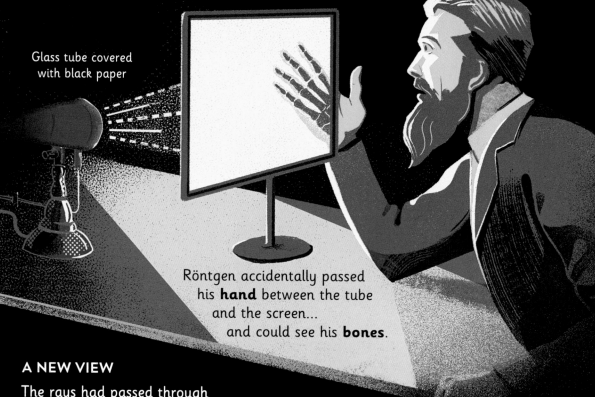

Glass tube covered with black paper

Röntgen accidentally passed his **hand** between the tube and the screen... and could see his **bones**.

A NEW VIEW

The rays had passed through the soft parts of his hand, but not through the dense bone. Röntgen decided to call the mysterious rays **X-rays** because "X" stands for something unknown.

Röntgen used X-rays to **photograph** his wife's hand. Immediately, he realized that **X-ray images** could be a valuable tool for doctors, and they have been used for looking inside patients' bodies ever since.

HOW FLO AND FRODO HELPED REVEAL
THE SECRET LIVES OF CHIMPS

Up until the 1960s, people thought that **chimpanzees** led simple, peaceful lives. One scientist's **in-depth study** of chimps changed all that...

In 1960, British biologist **Jane Goodall** started studying a group of **wild chimps** in Tanzania. Over years, she gave them **names** (including Flo and Frodo) and noticed some startling things.

For example, Goodall saw that chimps used **tools**, fishing termites from their nests with twigs...

...they showed **emotions**, by **hugging, kissing** and other gestures.

...they banded together to **hunt** other animals and **eat** their **meat**.

This **shocked** scientists, who thought only humans used tools, and that chimps were **peaceful vegetarians**.

By the 1980s, I realized that chimps are **in danger** from people **hunting** them and **destroying** their homes.

I've been **working** to **save** them ever since.

HOW A PHYSICIST INVENTED
THE FIRST BATTERY

In the late 1700s, most scientists thought electricity was a **mysterious force** generated by **living things**. Italian physicist and chemist **Alessandro Volta**, was the first to show that electricity was something that could be made using **simple** chemicals and equipment.

ITALY, 1797-1800

Through his experiments Volta found that two **different** metals connected by certain **liquids** would make a weak **electric current**. He tested various metals by dipping them in salt water and found that **zinc** and **copper** worked well together.

Next, he soaked pieces of cloth in salt water and placed them between discs of zinc and copper. He stacked them into a tall **pile** and found that, the more layers he added, the **stronger** the current he could make.

When I use this wire to **connect** the top of this pile to the bottom, an electric current **flows** through.

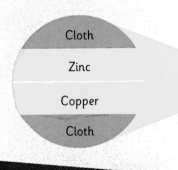

Cloth

Zinc

Copper

Cloth

By doing this, Volta had invented the **first battery.** Batteries quickly became the main way of making electricity, and are still vital for powering portable devices today.

FROM X-RAYS
TO RADIOACTIVITY

In 1895, Wilhelm Röntgen (see page 37) discovered **X-rays** – a mysterious type of energy given off by certain substances. Then, in 1896, Henri Becquerel discovered that an element called **uranium** seemed to give off similar rays. The race was on to find out more...

PARIS, 1896

Polish-born physicist **Marie Curie** started investigating uranium more closely. She suspected there might be similar elements that hadn't yet been discovered.

Curie took **rocks** that seemed to give off rays just as uranium did. She **crushed** and **heated** the rocks to separate out the parts that behaved like uranium.

JULY 1898

Curie discovered a **new element** that seemed to give off rays. She named it **polonium**, after her country of birth. Months later, she discovered another similar element, **radium**.

Po 84
POLONIUM

She invented the word "**radioactive**" for elements that seemed to give off rays – although it's now known they give off **particles**, not rays.

PRIZE TIME

In 1903 Curie won a **Nobel Prize for physics**, along with Pierre Curie, her husband who had worked alongside her on radioactivity, and Henri Becquerel.

Then, in 1911 she won a **Nobel Prize for chemistry** too, becoming the first person ever to win two Nobel Prizes.

Ra 88
RADIUM

A DEADLY DOSE

For most of this time, Curie worked **without protective** clothing, keeping radioactive substances in her pockets and desk drawers.

By 1934 she was ill with a condition caused by **exposure** to radioactivity. No one at the time knew how **deadly** radioactivity could be.

Even today, Curie's **notebooks** and **clothes** are so dangerously radioactive that they're **sealed** in lead-lined containers to prevent them from harming people.

USING EARTHQUAKES TO DISCOVER
EARTH'S INNER CORE

Before the 1930s, scientists believed that below the Earth's crust, the planet was made up of a **rocky mantle** and a **liquid core**. This all changed due to the logical reasoning and careful mathematics of Danish seismologist (earthquake scientist) **Inge Lehmann**.

NEW ZEALAND, 1929

A serious earthquake struck, sending vibrations known as **shock waves** around the world.

Earthquake

Crust

Mantle

Shock wave

UNEXPECTED EFFECTS

Lehmann expected the shock waves to travel through the crust and the mantle, then **bend** as they passed through the liquid core.

But the shock waves from New Zealand seemed to be **bouncing back** from part of the core. This made Lehmann wonder whether part of it might actually be **solid**.

Liquid outer core

Solid inner core

Lehmann published her idea, which was soon accepted by most scientists. They now think that the inner core is made mainly from the metals **iron** and **nickel**.

HOW RED LIGHT LED TO
BLUE AND WHITE

Many scientists worked together on Light Emitting Diodes (**LEDs**) – tiny lights used in everything from TV remote controls to fiberoptic cables. But just one scientist, **Shuji Nakamura**, made it possible for **blue** and **white** LEDs to be mass-produced...

THE FIRST LED...

In 1960s, scientists created the first efficient LED light by passing electricity through a material called gallium arsenide phosphide – a **semiconductor**. It glowed **red**.

...LED TO OTHERS

In the 1970s other semiconductors were found that glowed **yellow**, **green** or **blue**. But blue/green LEDs, using gallium nitride, were just too dim to be useful.

JAPAN, 1980s TO 1990s

Electronic engineer Nakamura worked with semiconductor scientists Isamu Akasaki and Hiroshi Amano. They made gallium nitride glow **bright blue**, but their method was too complex for mass-production.

In 1993 Nakamura found a way for factories to produce bright blue LEDs easily. Then, just by adding a **yellow coating**, he realized his blue LEDs could be turned **white**.

REWARDS

Bright white LEDS made **new technology** possible, including smartphone screens, LED TVs and low-energy LED lighting. In 2014 Nakamura, Akasaki and Amano shared a **Nobel Prize** for physics.

HOW A TELESCOPE ACCIDENTALLY REVEALED
EVIDENCE OF THE BIG BANG

In 1927, Georges Lemaître, a Belgian priest and physicist, suggested that **the Universe** began as a tiny single point that **exploded**, creating everything that exists in the Universe. This idea became known as **the Big Bang**. The first evidence for it was discovered accidentally, thanks to a telescope.

PICKING UP WAVES...

In 1964, American astronomers **Arno Allan Penzias** and **Robert Woodrow Wilson** started using a huge **telescope** that could pick up **waves** from distant parts of space.

...AND BUZZING

They noticed that the telescope detected a constant **buzz** that they couldn't explain. They thought it might be from radios in nearby New York City, but it wasn't.

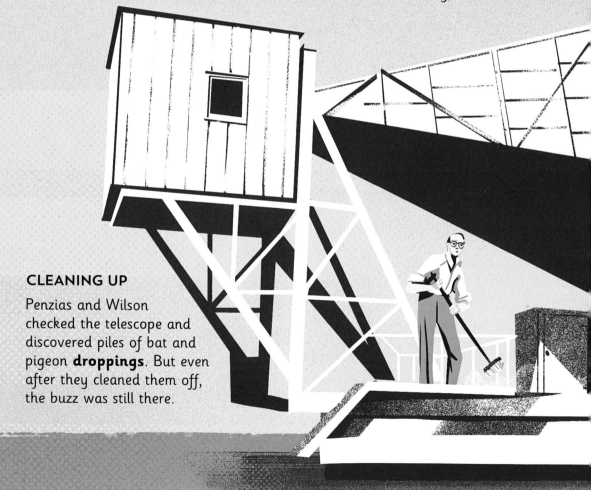

CLEANING UP

Penzias and Wilson checked the telescope and discovered piles of bat and pigeon **droppings**. But even after they cleaned them off, the buzz was still there.

COSMIC MICROWAVE BACKGROUND

It gradually dawned on Penzias and Wilson that the buzz might be very faint **radiation** left over from the Big Bang. Other physicists were already looking for this radiation, which they called **Cosmic Microwave Background**, or CMB.

CONFIRMATION

When Penzias and Wilson published their results, other scientists agreed they really had discovered CMB. This was the first **direct evidence** for the Big Bang.

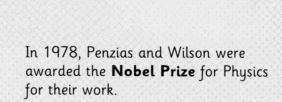

In 1978, Penzias and Wilson were awarded the **Nobel Prize** for Physics for their work.

HOW HISTORY WAS CHANGED BY
ONE QUICK PHONE CALL

March 10, 1876 became one of the most important dates in the history of science, when Scottish inventor **Alexander Graham Bell** made the first ever telephone call.

Several scientists had been working on ways to **transmit speech** from one place to another, but Bell was the first to succeed. He built a device that turned **vibrations** caused by sound into **electricity**, and then back into sound.

Bell spoke into the top of the device. The sound made a drum inside vibrate, causing changes in an electric current.

The current flowed along a wire.

The changing current caused a reed to vibrate in the receiver instrument, turning it back into sound.

Bell made this **first successful transmission of speech** to his assistant Thomas Watson. He said:

Mr. Watson, come here. I want to see you.

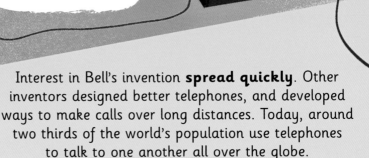

Interest in Bell's invention **spread quickly**. Other inventors designed better telephones, and developed ways to make calls over long distances. Today, around two thirds of the world's population use telephones to talk to one another all over the globe.

THE BOTANIST
WHO EXPLORED THE AMAZON

Most modern scientists' careers lead straight from school to university, then research. But one Mexican-American **botanist** named **Ynes Mexia** didn't embark on her scientific journey until she was 55. Despite this, she collected more than 500 previously undiscovered plant species, and had 50 named after her.

THE ADVENTURE BEGINS

In 1925, Mexia set off to western **Mexico** to collect wild plants.

She gathered more than **500 plants** on that trip.

OVER THE NEXT 13 YEARS...

Mexia collected thousands of plants in the most remote locations – from Alaska to the southern tip of Chile. She even spent two and a half years exploring the entire length of the **Amazon River**.

AND BEYOND...

Mexia sent everything she found to **universities**. Almost 100 years after her first trip, botanists are still **examining** and **classifying** her finds.

DIGGING UP NEW IDEAS ABOUT
LIFE ON EARTH

Only 200 years ago, no one knew dinosaurs and other prehistoric creatures had ever existed. One woman, **Mary Anning**, made discoveries that helped change all that...

In 1810, when she was just 11 years old, Anning took over her family business — selling **fossils** she found on the beaches of **Lyme Regis**, in the south of England. She scoured the steep cliffs, cracking open rocks, hunting for **prehistoric** "curiosities" to sell.

PAST LIVES

Ichthyosaur

In 1812, Anning discovered the skeleton of a long reptile with sharp teeth. It was a creature **no one knew had existed** until then, but it's now called an **ichthyosaur**, meaning fish-lizard.

The ichthyosaur helped prove a theory that there were once animals on Earth that had since **died out**.

Anning continued to hunt for fossils for 35 years. She discovered **hundreds**, including those of flying reptiles called **pterosaurs**...

Pterosaur

...and long-necked swimming **plesiosaurs**.

Plesiosaur

In those days, women were discouraged from publishing books or articles, so Anning's work went unnoticed. But today she's recognized as one of the greatest ever **paleontologists**.

HOW SEA URCHINS
CHANGED THE WAY BIOLOGISTS WORK

Around 1900, most biologists assumed that **cells** – tiny building blocks that make up all living things – behave the same way in a **laboratory** as they do in **nature**. In fact, some cells react very differently in the artificial conditions of a lab, as one scientist pointed out...

AMERICA, 1907

Ernest Everett Just graduated from Dartmouth College, one of America's most prestigious universities. He was a brilliant student and won many **prizes**.

He decided to become a **marine biologist** and experimented with living **egg cells** from sea creatures including **sea urchins** and **sand dollars**. He discovered completely new things about the way egg cells develop.

By working with cells both in the **sea** and in a **lab**, he managed to prove that biologists must make lab conditions as **natural** as possible, or their results might not be reliable.

We feel the beauty of nature because we are part of nature.

Ernest Everett Just's research didn't receive much recognition in his lifetime, but scientists today realize how **valuable** it was.

THE DOCTOR WHO WROTE
THE MEDICAL RULE BOOK

In ancient times, scientists from different cultures built up their own knowledge and different ideas about medicine. Then, around a thousand years ago, a Persian doctor named **Ibn Sina** attempted to bring many of these together into one encyclopedic book.

STUDY TOURS

Ibn Sina read and studied widely. He toured around the **Middle East**, **Greece**, **India** and **China**, learning about as many different **medical systems** as he could.

Medicinal substances

Chemistry

Surgery

Anatomy

ENCYCLOPEDIC KNOWLEDGE

By 1025 he had completed *The Canon of Medicine*, a book recording all the knowledge he had collected. In the **12th century**, the book found its way to Europe, where Ibn Sina was known as **Avicenna**. His book soon became the standard medical textbook and would remain so for over 500 years.

HOW BOILING A BROTH PROVED THAT
GERMS MAKE FOOD GO BAD

While investigating why food and drinks go bad, French chemist **Louis Pasteur** came to believe that tiny living things known as **microbes** or **germs** were the cause. To prove his theory, he performed an experiment...

Pasteur boiled a meat broth in a flask to **kill** any germs already present. This created a completely **sterile** (clean) environment.

He then **sealed** the flask to stop new germs from getting in. He left it for a **year** and the broth didn't go bad.

Pasteur then **removed the lid** so new germs could get in. Within a **day** the liquid became cloudy and the broth went bad. Under a microscope he could see it was **filled** with germs.

GOING FURTHER...

In 1862 Pasteur developed a heating process that stopped things such as milk from going bad so quickly. The process is called **pasteurization** after him.

Pasteur went on to help prove that germs cause diseases in people too. This understanding has saved countless lives.

A MATHEMATICAL GENIUS
WHOSE IDEAS WERE FAR AHEAD OF HIS TIME

Every now and then a mathematical genius comes along — someone whose ideas are so far **ahead of their time** that many decades pass before they're properly appreciated and understood. **Srinivasa Ramanujan** was one of these geniuses.

INDIA, 1900s

Ramanujan won **school prizes** for mathematics, but struggled to find a job. He spent his spare time filling notebooks with mathematical **ideas** and **formulas**.

A BREAKTHROUGH

In 1913, Ramanujan wrote to several mathematicians at Cambridge University in Britain. One of them, G.H. Hardy, saw his outstanding abilities and offered him a **job**.

Ramanujan moved to Cambridge and **published** some of his ideas.

In 1918 he was made a Fellow of the **Royal Society** — one of the highest scientific accolades.

CUT SHORT

Sadly, in 1920, Ramanujan died, at just **32 years old**. He had not yet had a chance to publish many of his most brilliant mathematical ideas.

But Ramanujan's ideas live on in his **letters** and **notebooks**. They're now helping to explain things such as how **black holes** work. A number has even been named after Ramanujan and his tutor Hardy.

The **Hardy-Ramanujan number** is 1729. This number has some features that make it of interest to mathematicians. Ramanujan was the first to point out these features after Hardy spotted the number on a taxi.

1729

HOW A MIRROR AND A LAMP
SHED LIGHT ON A MOON MYSTERY

Throughout history, people have been puzzled by **lunar eclipses** – times when a **shadow** falls across the **Moon**. Some people tried to explain lunar eclipses with stories about magical creatures eating the Moon. But, around 300 years ago, a lone scientist discovered the **real reason**...

CHINA, AROUND 1780-1790

A woman named **Wang Zhenyi** studied the writings of earlier scientists who had recorded the positions of the Sun, Earth and Moon during eclipses.

BUILD AND TEST

Wang Zhenyi decided to build a **model** to test what was really happening during eclipses. She found a round **table** to represent the Earth, placed a round **mirror**, for the Moon, next to it, and hung up a **lamp** to act as the Sun.

By moving the lamp, table and mirror to different positions, she saw that an eclipse happens on rare occasions when the Earth is **between** the Sun and the Moon. It's the Sun casting a **shadow** of the Earth across the Moon that causes a lunar eclipse.

Wang Zhenyi wrote down her findings in a **book** – just one of several she wrote. In 2004, to celebrate her outstanding achievements, an area on the **planet Venus** was named after her.

THE SCIENTIST WHO GAVE HIS NAME
TO HALF A GAS CLOUD

Many people have heard of a particle called a **boson**, but few know that it was named after Indian physicist **Satyendra Nath Bose**. His name is also used alongside Einstein's to describe a type of **gas cloud** with amazing properties...

HELLO EINSTEIN

In 1924, Bose wrote a letter to famous physicist Albert Einstein (see page 12) pointing out that the **mathematics** behind one of Einstein's theories didn't match **evidence** from experiments.

CHANGING THE RULES

Bose proposed a **new** type of **calculation**. Einstein agreed that this solved the problem. He realized Bose's idea meant that — in some groups of particles — it's impossible to tell which particle is which. These particles are now named **bosons** after Bose.

Laser

Bose-Einstein condensate

CLOUDING OVER

Einstein also imagined a **cloud** of super-cooled gas where all the particles behave identically. He called this a **Bose-Einstein condensate**

In 1995, scientists created a Bose-Einstein condensate cloud for the first time ever, using **lasers** and **magnets**

HOW TO DO PHYSICS AT
THE SPEED OF LIGHT

Light travels through space at 300,000km (around 186,000 miles) per second. That's **really, really fast**. But one scientist managed to slow it down, and even stop it completely – Danish physicist **Lene Hau**.

AMERICA, 1997

Hau led a team **firing light** into a Bose-Einstein condensate. The light slowed down as it passed through the cloud. This wasn't surprising – light always slows a little as it passes through things, but...

Magnet

...by adjusting her equipment, Hau managed to slow the light down **a lot** – to just 60km (37 miles) per hour. That's around the speed of a bicycle. This was the **slowest speed** ever recorded for light.

Magnet

Cooling laser

COMING TO A STOP

Then, in 2001, Hau made a pulse of light **stop** inside the cloud for one thousandth of a second. She was the first ever person to do this – achieving what

HARNESSING THE ENERGY
INSIDE ATOMS

In the 1920s and 30s, people were beginning to realize that **atoms** — the tiny particles that make up almost everything — had vast amounts of **energy** inside them. The next step was to find out how to **release** that energy...

ITALY, 1934

Physicist **Enrico Fermi** had been the first to point out that Einstein's theory of **Special Relativity** (see page 13) meant that vast amounts of **energy** could be **released** by splitting atoms.

Fermi found he could change the properties of atoms by **bombarding** them with even smaller particles. This won him a **Nobel Prize**. He only discovered later that what he had actually done was to **split atoms**.

This is **Chicago Pile-1** – the first nuclear reactor.

AMERICA, 1942

Fermi led a team of scientists building the first **nuclear reactor** — equipment designed to split atoms and **capture the energy** they released.

It was based on the idea that when one atom splits, it fires out particles that then split nearby atoms, that then split more atoms, and so on. Fermi's reactor produced only a **tiny amount** of power, but it proved that it could work.

Today, nuclear reactors harness the power of atoms and use it to make around **10%** of the **world's electricity**. And they do all this using the same atom-splitting science that Fermi demonstrated more than 75 years ago.

JOINING THE NATURAL WORLD
BACK TOGETHER AGAIN

By the 1790s, scientists had **divided up** the natural world into different subject areas. Usually, each scientist chose to specialize in just one subject. But one scientist decided to look at nature as a **whole**, to try to see the bigger picture...

SMALL START...

German naturalist **Alexander von Humboldt** was fascinated by shells, plants and insects, even as a child. In his twenties, he toured parts of Europe, studying plants, rocks and the landscape.

...TO BIG ADVENTURE

In 1799, Humboldt **set sail** for South America. It changed his view of the world.

Humboldt recorded hundreds of **new** types of **plants** and **animals**, and heaps of **data** about the **weather**, **rocks** and **people** he saw.

TREE TROUBLE

In Venezuela he saw the disastrous effect **cutting down trees** had on the environment, and became the first scientist to talk about **climate change** caused by people.

JOINING IT UP

His voyage led Humboldt to see nature as a complex, **interconnected ecosystem**. His ideas later influenced Charles Darwin (see page 32) and other scientists.

I must find out about the unity of nature.

HOW AN ARTIST SPREAD HER WINGS
AND BECAME A SCIENTIST

In 1669, Dutch scientist Jan Swammerdam proved that **insects** went through **different stages** in their lives, for example, from egg to caterpillar to butterfly. People had previously thought these stages were just different animals. But it was left to an artist-turned-scientist to research insect **life cycles** in detail...

GERMANY, 1679

A professional artist who studied insects in her spare time, **Maria Sybilla Merian**, published a book about insect life cycles. She went on to publish many more.

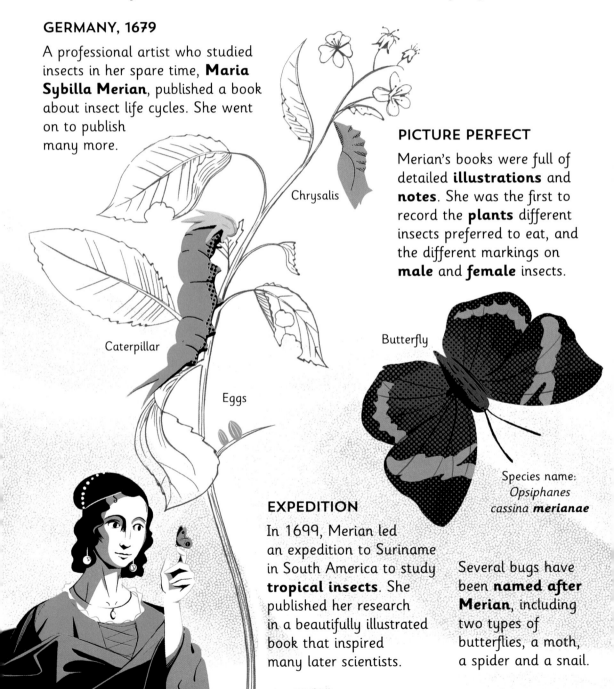

Chrysalis

PICTURE PERFECT

Merian's books were full of detailed **illustrations** and **notes**. She was the first to record the **plants** different insects preferred to eat, and the different markings on **male** and **female** insects.

Caterpillar

Butterfly

Eggs

Species name:
Opsiphanes cassina **merianae**

EXPEDITION

In 1699, Merian led an expedition to Suriname in South America to study **tropical insects**. She published her research in a beautifully illustrated book that inspired many later scientists.

Several bugs have been **named after Merian**, including two types of butterflies, a moth, a spider and a snail.

HOW A DOCTOR PROVED THAT SOME
BACTERIA ARE DEADLY

It was not until the 1860s that most scientists realized that **bacteria** – tiny, single-celled living things – can cause **disease**. In the 1880s, one scientist took this further, pinpointing the bacteria that cause two **deadly** diseases: **anthrax** and **tuberculosis**.

GERMANY, 1880

Doctor and biologist **Robert Koch** set out to track down the **exact** bacteria that caused particular diseases.

Koch collected bacteria from sick patients and grew them in round dishes on a type of **gel** called **agar**. Then, he infected **guinea pigs** with the bacteria he'd grown.

If a guinea pig became ill, Koch collected **new bacteria** from it and grew them. If the new bacteria matched the **original bacteria**, Koch knew he had found the cause of the disease.

Koch's **breakthrough** led to advances in medicine that saved countless lives. His methods of matching bacteria to find the causes of **infectious diseases**, and of **growing bacteria** in gel, are still used today.

HOW AN ASTRONOMER REDREW THE
MAP OF THE UNIVERSE...

At the start of the 16th century, most people believed that the **Earth** was at the **middle** of the **Universe**, and that the Sun, Moon and other planets all moved in circles around it. One astronomer, though, had a very different idea...

OBSERVING THE NIGHT SKY

Polish astronomer, **Nicolaus Copernicus**, carefully studied the movements of the **Moon and planets**, and started to form a new picture of the Universe...

In 1532, Copernicus completed his theory: the Universe doesn't revolve around the Earth; instead the Earth **orbits** the **Sun**.

Saturn

Jupiter

Venus

Sun

Mercury

Moon

Earth

Mars

The solar system according to Copernicus

When my theory came out, a lot of people were **shocked** and **angry** at the idea that Earth was just an **ordinary planet**.

Later astronomers proved that Copernicus's ideas were correct. Today, his map of the **solar system** is known as the **Copernican model**.

... AND A SCIENTIST MAPPED
THE HUMAN BRAIN

After many years of research the human brain still holds many mysteries. But one seemingly simple question — how do humans find their way around? — has now been answered.

FROM RAT BRAINS...

Many discoveries about how the human brain works have come from studying rats' brains first. In 2005, Norwegian neuroscientist **May-Britt Moser**, and her then husband Edvard, began working with rats.

Moser monitored the rats' **brain activity** as they explored a **new environment**. She saw that certain cells in an area of the brain known as the **temporal lobe** became very **active**.

The activity of these cells created a **grid-like map** within the brain, allowing the rats to remember where they had been, and the way from one point to another.

Because of the grid the cells created, I named them **grid cells**.

TO HUMAN BRAINS...

Further research found that humans also have grid cells. Moser is now using this discovery to conduct research into memory-related illnesses such as **Alzheimer's disease**.

FULL STEAM AHEAD
TO SOME INCREDIBLE INVENTIONS

In the 18th century, engineers in Britain began working on ways to use **steam** to power engines. In 1712, English ironmonger Thomas Newcomen built a steam engine to pump water from mines. Then, in 1769, Scottish inventor James Watt built a more efficient version, to power factories and turn wheels. Cornish mining engineer **Richard Trevithick** went further...

1797

Trevithick designed an engine that used steam at a **higher pressure** than Watt's engine, which meant it could be smaller and lighter.

1801

Trevithick made **Puffing Devil** – the first ever **steam-powered vehicle**. On Christmas Eve he rode it with some friends up a hill in Camborne, Cornwall.

1804

Trevithick built a steam **locomotive** – an engine that pulls a load along rails. On February 21, it hauled 70 people for ten miles.

Later, engineers such as Robert Stephenson built locomotives that were able to pull loads much further and at faster speeds. But Trevithick is still considered the **inventor of steam locomotion**.

AN ENTERTAINING INVENTION
THAT WAS ALSO A LIFE-SAVER

In 1888, German physicist Heinrich Hertz proved the existence of what we now call **radio waves**. But Hertz thought these waves were useless. It took another brilliant scientist to invent a workable **wireless communication system** based on them...

ITALY, 1894

A young electrical engineer, **Guglielmo Marconi,** rigged up a **transmitter** that sent radio waves as a signal to a **receiver** on the other side of the room.

Marconi worked hard to **strengthen** the signal. By 1895, he was able to receive radio signals from 3.2km (2 miles) away.

By the early 1900s, Marconi could transmit radio signals more than 4,000km (2,500 miles) across the Atlantic Ocean. In 1909, he won a **Nobel Prize** for Physics.

By the 1920s, my invention started a **golden age of radio**, with news and entertainment broadcast worldwide. Radio had already **saved lives**, too, enabling ships in trouble (including the **Titanic**) to call for help.

STUDYING ANCIENT TEXTS REVEALED
HOW TO TREAT MALARIA

Malaria, which is passed on by mosquito bites, is one of the **world's deadliest diseases**. Half the world's population is at risk of catching it. In 1969, the Chinese government gave a chemist named **Tu Youyou** the task of finding a treatment...

ANCIENT KNOWLEDGE

Tu Youyou started by studying ancient Chinese texts that listed the medical properties of different plants and herbs. Eventually, she came across one that advised using a herb called **sweet wormwood** to treat recurring fevers – a common sign of malaria.

With the help of the 1,600-year-old medical text, Tu Youyou successfully extracted something known as **artemisinin** from the wormwood.

TESTING IT OUT

Tu Youyou found artemisinin was effective when used to treat mice and monkeys. To be sure it would work on humans too, she **tested it on herself**. It was a success and her work was published, but for years no one outside Asia knew it existed. In 1981, news of Tu Youyou's treatment spread and companies began mass-producing it.

In 2015, Tu Youyou was awarded a **Nobel Prize** for her incredible work, which has already saved **millions** of lives.

Every scientist dreams of doing something that can help the world.

HOW A LITTLE PEBBLE
MADE BIG WAVES

For centuries, mathematicians puzzled over how to make tricky calculations, such as the area of a wavy shape. Then, in the 1670s, German mathematician and thinker **Gottfried Leibniz** found a way. He created a type of mathematics known as *calculus* – a Latin word used to describe a little pebble used for adding.

Leibniz wanted to calculate the amount of space a wavy shape took up on a graph – its **area**. Previous mathematicians had shown how to get a **rough** answer, but Leibniz wanted to be **accurate**.

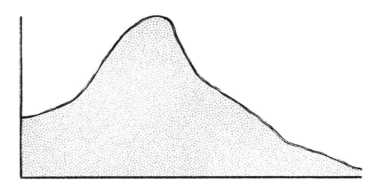

First, he came up with **mathematical formulas** for splitting up the shape into **smaller and smaller** shapes. These areas could be calculated more easily. Then, he added these together to find the total area.

Leibniz spent years working on his formulas, choosing **symbols** that would be easy to understand. He finally **published** his ideas in 1684. Two years later, Isaac Newton (see page 72) claimed Leibniz had stolen the idea of calculus from him. It's now agreed Leibniz discovered it on his own.

HOW SECRET WARTIME CODES REVEALED
A COMPUTING GENIUS

During the Second World War, different **code-breaking machines** were created by several remarkable scientists. One of these scientists was **Alan Turing**, a British mathematician so far ahead of his time that he wrote about **computers** before they even existed. His code-breaking machine brought computers one step closer.

BEGINNINGS

Turing first published his ideas about computers in 1936, calling them **Turing machines** – though at that time they existed only in his imagination. When the Second World War broke out in 1939, Turing went to work for the British military, cracking **codes** used by their enemies, the Germans.

These codes had been created using devices called **Enigma machines**. Inspired by a Polish code-breaking machine, Turing designed the **Bombe** – a machine with hundreds of rotating cylinders powered by **electricity**.

BRILLIANT BOMBE

The Bombe **decoded** Enigma messages quickly. Historians believe this may have **shortened the war** by two years and **saved** as many as **14 million lives**.

More than this, Turing's **ideas** about computers have gone on to influence generations of **computer scientists**.

A COLOSSAL EFFORT
BUILT THE VERY FIRST COMPUTER

The first ever **programmable electronic computer** was nicknamed **Colossus**, and cracked the most difficult codes invented during the Second World War. It was designed and built by a British engineer named **Tommy Flowers**.

SETTING TO WORK

In 1943, Flowers was asked to design a machine to crack a very complex German code – the **Lorenz cipher**. Alan Turing and other code-breakers had found a slow, long-hand method for breaking the cipher, but needed a machine to speed things up.

Flowers worked on a machine that used **electrical circuits** made from glass **vacuum tubes**. These weren't always dependable, but Flowers believed he could build a more powerful, reliable machine using thousands of vacuum tubes.

JUST IN TIME

The code-breakers dismissed Flowers' idea, but he continued, designing and building a **vast machine** named **Colossus**. It worked. Then, in 1944 an upgraded version of it broke codes relating to the D-Day landings – operations that **changed the course of the war**.

Colossus was the **world's first** programmable, electronic, digital computer. At the end of the war, Flowers was ordered to **destroy** it, to protect national security. So, his contribution to computing went unrecognized for many years.

67

PUT THE WORLD IN ORDER

in the 1860s, Russian chemist **Dmitri Mendeleev** had a dream about — the basic chemical substances that make up everything on the planet. voke he drew a diagram that **grouped** elements with similar properties. as the **Periodic Table**, and it now forms the basis of all chemistry.

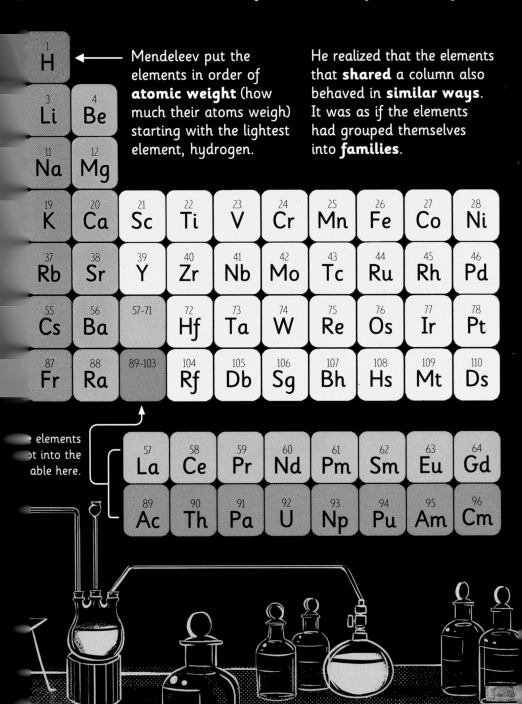

Mendeleev put the elements in order of **atomic weight** (how much their atoms weigh) starting with the lightest element, hydrogen.

He realized that the elements that **shared** a column also behaved in **similar ways**. It was as if the elements had grouped themselves into **families**.

1 H									
3 Li	4 Be								
11 Na	12 Mg								
19 K	20 Ca	21 Sc	22 Ti	23 V	24 Cr	25 Mn	26 Fe	27 Co	28 Ni
37 Rb	38 Sr	39 Y	40 Zr	41 Nb	42 Mo	43 Tc	44 Ru	45 Rh	46 Pd
55 Cs	56 Ba	57-71	72 Hf	73 Ta	74 W	75 Re	76 Os	77 Ir	78 Pt
87 Fr	88 Ra	89-103	104 Rf	105 Db	106 Sg	107 Bh	108 Hs	109 Mt	110 Ds

e elements
t into the
able here.

57 La	58 Ce	59 Pr	60 Nd	61 Pm	62 Sm	63 Eu	64 Gd
89 Ac	90 Th	91 Pa	92 U	93 Np	94 Pu	95 Am	96 Cm

Only **56** of the elements shown here had been discovered when Mendeleev set out his table, but he was so sure that others would fit this pattern that he left **gaps** for them.

Sure enough, the missing elements were soon found and the table extended. Today there are **118** elements in the Periodic Table, and what Mendeleev called atomic weight is understood as atomic mass.

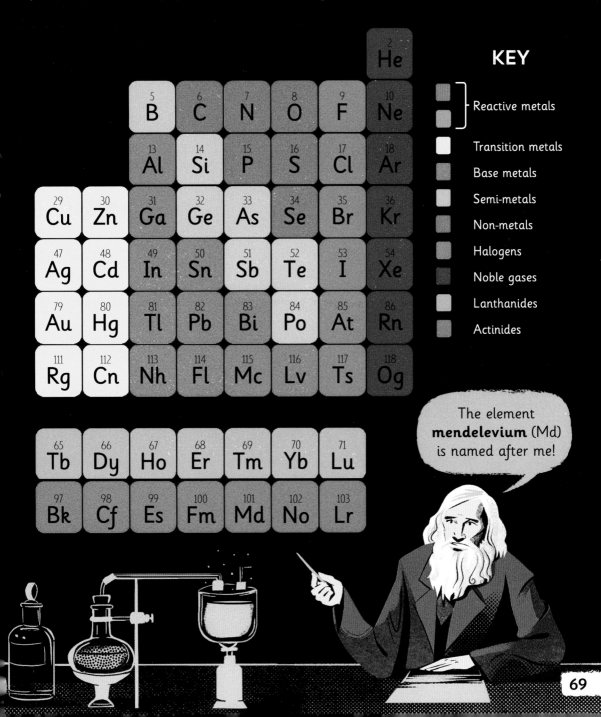

KEY

- Reactive metals
- Transition metals
- Base metals
- Semi-metals
- Non-metals
- Halogens
- Noble gases
- Lanthanides
- Actinides

The element **mendelevium** (Md) is named after me!

DISCOVERING GALAXIES
FAR, FAR AWAY

Less than 100 years ago, astronomers thought that our **galaxy**, the Milky Way, was the whole **Universe**. One astronomer showed that, really, there was much more out there...

CALIFORNIA, AMERICA, 1919

Astronomer **Edwin Hubble** began working at Mount Wilson Observatory. Studying light from a far-off star, he calculated that it came from beyond the **Milky Way.** This proved there must be **other galaxies** out there...

Hubble discovered that the other galaxies were **moving away** from us. The greater the distance between them, the faster they were moving – this became known as **Hubble's Law**.

Lots of things in space are named after Hubble, including an asteroid, a crater on the Moon, and the **Hubble Space Telescope**, which has orbited Earth since 1990, taking incredible photos of **distant galaxies**.

LATER THEORIES

Hubble's work backed up the theory that the Universe is **expanding**, and that all matter was once packed together, until it exploded outwards – an event called **the Big Bang**.

Some scientists use equipment that collides **subatomic particles** called electrons and positrons together. This can create very unusual particles, including different types of **mesons**, as one scientist discovered...

JAPAN, 2003

South Korean physicist **Sookyung Choi** was working with others including her colleague Stephen Olsen, using particle-colliding equipment known as **KEKB**.

Path of particles

One day, when some particles **collided**, Choi noticed traces of a **meson** — but it wasn't a type anyone had spotted before.

Most mesons are made from two even tinier particles, a **quark** and an **anti-quark**. But this was an **exotic meson**, which scientists had predicted as early as 1961, suggesting they are made from a quark, an anti-quark, and **at least** one extra, **unknown**, particle.

My exotic meson — named **X(3872)** — was the first one ever detected.

Choi suggested that the extra particle or particles in X(3872) might be a **gluon** (a particle that glues quarks together) or two (or even three) additional **quarks**. This is still the best explanation, but no one yet knows exactly how X(3872) works.

HOW A FALLING APPLE
CHANGED SCIENCE FOREVER

In the 1700s in Europe, a series of major developments took place that became known as the **Scientific Revolution**. One of the most influential scientists of this exciting period was a British mathematician, physicist and astronomer named **Isaac Newton**.

RETURNING FROM COLLEGE

In 1665, promising student Isaac Newton had to leave university, after his college closed because of an outbreak of plague. He returned to his family's farm in the north of England.

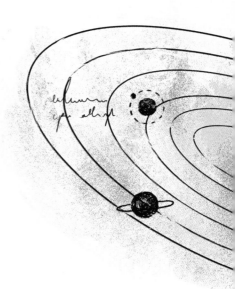

A REVELATION

One story says that seeing an **apple** fall from a tree made Newton think about **gravity** – the force that pulls objects to the ground...

I realized that all objects have a **gravitational pull** on each other, and that the same force holds the Moon in orbit around Earth, and the planets around the Sun.

LOOKING INTO LIGHT

Newton grew fascinated by light, too. Scientists believed that **white light** was a single entity, but Newton thought there was more to it.

He passed a beam of sunlight through a **prism**, and found that the light split into rays of red, orange, yellow, green, blue, indigo and violet. What he'd discovered was that white light was made of all these rays combined.

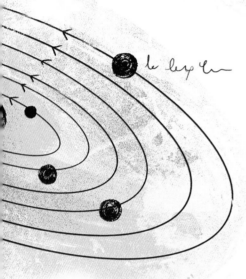

MIRRORS AND MATHEMATICS

Newton designed a powerful **telescope** that used mirrors, instead of lenses, to **reflect light**. He also developed a way to solve complex mathematical problems, a form of **calculus** similar to that created by Gottfried Leibniz (see page 65).

THREE LAWS OF MOTION

In 1687, Newton published **Philosophiae Naturalis Principia Mathematica** – a book that changed science forever. It set out three laws to describe how and why objects move. Newton's **Three Laws of Motion** explain the forces that make the **whole Universe work**, and form the foundation of modern physics.

THE DOCTOR WHO DISCOVERED
BLOOD GROUPS

Before the 20th century, **blood transfusions** – when a patient who has lost blood is given some from another person – sometimes made a patient completely better, but often caused severe **illness** or **death**. But no one knew why. Then in 1900, an Austrian doctor, **Karl Landsteiner**, found the answer...

VIENNA, 1900

Landsteiner became interested in **blood serum** – a pale yellow liquid that carries red blood cells around the body.

Landsteiner took serum from one person and **mixed** it with red blood cells from someone else. He saw that this often caused the red blood cells to **clump** together – something that can prove **fatal**.

He continued his experiments, and found that *some* combinations of serum and blood caused clumping, but *others* didn't. He concluded that people must have **different types** of blood.

Landsteiner identified three **blood groups** that he referred to as **A**, **B** and **C**. (C is now known as **O**.)

Landsteiner found that, if he mixed the blood of two people with the **same** blood group, there would be no clumping of red blood cells.

This discovery meant that doctors could test their patients' blood to find out their blood group and then give them safe blood transfusions. **Millions** of lives are saved every year thanks to blood transfusions.

FROM AMATEUR ASTRONOMER TO
SUNSPOT SPOTTER

For thousands of years, scientists have observed and recorded darker patches, known as **sunspots**, that appear and disappear on the surface of the Sun. But one astronomer kept a detailed record like no other...

TOKYO, JAPAN, 1940s

During the Second World War, the Tokyo authorities ordered blackouts to prevent enemy pilots from bombing the city. One amateur astronomer, **Hisako Koyama**, took advantage of the darkness to go out stargazing.

Koyama soon started observing the **Sun** too. To avoid damaging her eyes, she used her telescope to project the image of the Sun onto a piece of paper, then sketched what she saw.

In 1946, Koyama began working at the National Museum of Nature and Science in Tokyo. Every day for the next **40 years**, she drew and made notes about sunspots, building up an archive of more than **10,000 drawings**.

UNDERSTANDING SUNSPOTS

Scientists now know that sunspots are a sign of powerful **magnetic surges** on the Sun that can cause changes to Earth's atmosphere and disrupt satellite and radio signals.

Koyama's notes have provided experts with a valuable record of past **patterns** and **cycles** in the Sun's activity that help them to **predict** how the Sun might affect life on Earth in the future.

THE ASTRONOMER WHO DISCOVERED THE
COMPOSITION OF THE STARS

Before 1925, astronomers thought that **stars** were all made up of exactly the same chemical **elements,** in the exact same **quantities,** as planet Earth. Thanks to one gifted astronomer, **Cecilia Payne-Gaposchkin**, we now know this is not the case.

FROM STUDENT...

In 1923, Gaposchkin graduated from Cambridge University, in Britain. She went to the US to study at **Harvard College Observatory**.

By comparing **light** given off by different stars, Gaposchkin was able to calculate the **elements** contained within them. She found that stars are mainly made of the gases **hydrogen** and **helium**.

"The reward of the young scientist is the emotional thrill of being the first person in the history of the world to understand something."

Her supervisors thought this was **impossible**. They were adamant — stars could not be made of gas. She was told not to publish her findings. But, in 1929, four years after her discovery, she was proved to be **correct**.

...TO TEACHER

When Gaposchkin started out, very few women taught in universities. In 1956, she became the **first female professor** at Harvard University, making further important discoveries and inspiring other women to follow scientific careers.

AMAZING NEW IDEAS THAT CAME FROM
A DREAM POOL

Around 1,000 years ago, in China, a government official named **Shen Kuo** made discoveries that were hundreds of years ahead of scientists elsewhere. In 1088, he retired to a country home called Dream Pool and wrote a book, ***Dream Pool Essays***.

In it, he included...

...detailed information about **animals** and **plants** he'd seen, including crocodiles and giant clams...

...a theory on how **rainbows** form...

...the first description of a **magnetic compass**, suggesting that its needle doesn't point directly north, but to a magnetic force in the **north**...

...the earliest account of **printing** using carved blocks, which was invented in China around the year 1,000...

...and the first record of what he believed to be a **U.F.O.** — mysterious lights in the night sky.

His book also included a new idea that the stars and planets were **spheres**, and the Moon **reflected**, rather than created, light...

...the first suggestion that the Earth goes through **climate change**...

...and a study of **seashells**, which led to his theory that coasts are worn away by the sea.

DISCOVERING THE DEADLY TRUTH ABOUT
DANGEROUS PESTICIDES

In the 1940s, many scientists worked on developing chemicals known as **pesticides**, to kill bugs that destroyed farmers' crops, or spread deadly diseases. But some of these pesticides were **killing fish, birds** and maybe even **people**, too. One scientist had the courage to stand up against her colleagues.

AMERICA, 1940s

Biologist **Rachel Carson** became worried about widespread use of a pesticide known as **DDT**.

Some reports showed that DDT didn't only kill pests, but also other plants and insects, plus birds and fish that had eaten those plants or insects. There were hints that DDT was making people sick, too.

SPEAKING OUT

Carson collected the evidence in a book called **Silent Spring**, published in 1962.

UNDER ATTACK

Chemical companies (who made DDT) attacked Carson's book — but many **scientists** supported it.

In 1963 Carson gave **evidence** to the US government about the dangers of DDT, but it took 10 years for DDT to be **banned** in America, and even longer in other countries.

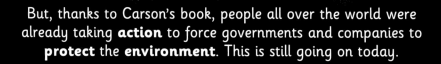

But, thanks to Carson's book, people all over the world were already taking **action** to force governments and companies to **protect** the **environment**. This is still going on today.

HOW A SCIENTIST FROM A CHILLY CLIMATE
PREDICTED GLOBAL WARMING

In the 1870s, scientists knew that Earth had experienced **ice ages** – periods of **global cooling** – but not **why**. To try to solve the problem, one scientist looked into the past, and saw the future...

Swedish chemist **Svante Arrhenius** was best known at the time for his work on acids and bases. But he became fascinated by the theory that historical global cooling had been caused by decreases in **carbon dioxide** in the atmosphere. He made thousands of calculations and proved this was correct.

Arrhenius predicted that factories burning **coal and gas** would cause a significant **increase** in carbon dioxide in Earth's atmosphere. This would result in **global warming**.

At the time, Arrhenius **wasn't too alarmed**. He noted that global warming might lead to much **nicer** weather in his chilly home country, Sweden.

Arrhenius **published** his research in 1896, but few scientists paid it much attention. It wasn't until the 1970s that the **threat of global warming** predicted in Arrhenius's work was taken seriously.

A BRAND NEW WAY
OF DESIGNING DRUGS

Up to the 1950s, scientists looking for **new drugs** to treat diseases simply tried out many different drugs, hoping some might work. But one scientist had a very **different** approach...

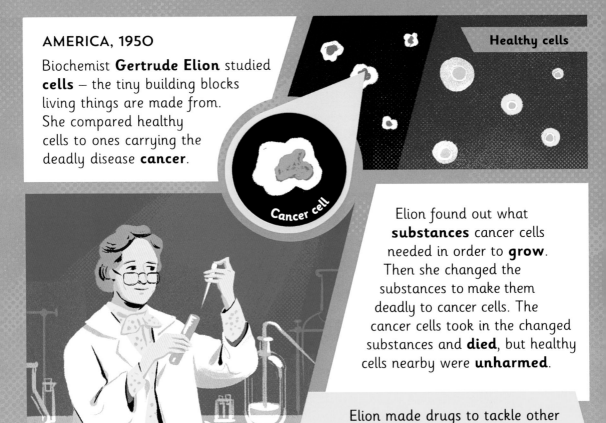

AMERICA, 1950

Biochemist **Gertrude Elion** studied **cells** – the tiny building blocks living things are made from. She compared healthy cells to ones carrying the deadly disease **cancer**.

Healthy cells

Cancer cell

Elion found out what **substances** cancer cells needed in order to **grow**. Then she changed the substances to make them deadly to cancer cells. The cancer cells took in the changed substances and **died**, but healthy cells nearby were **unharmed**.

Elion made drugs to tackle other life-threatening **diseases**, too.

THEN, IN 1957...

Elion made a drug that tricked patients' cells into **accepting** body parts **transplanted** from another person. Before this, transplant patients had died because their cells **rejected** the new part. Elion's drug made many transplants **successful.**

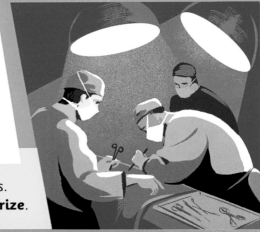

Elion's research saved countless lives. In 1988, she was awarded a **Nobel Prize**.

THE SCIENTIST WHO FIXED PROBLEMS
WITH PEANUTS

Around 1900, the main crop in the southern states in America was cotton. But it left the soil poor and the farmers poorer. Scientists knew some of the answers, but they weren't explaining them to the farmers. That is, until **George Washington Carver** came along...

GROWING A SCIENTIST

Carver was born a slave. Even after slavery ended, he had to fight for a good schooling. He studied **botany** (plants) and **agriculture** (farming) at Iowa State University, where he was the first African-American student and then the first African-American teacher.

Cotton plant

Peanut plant

ALABAMA, SOUTHERN US, 1896

Carver became head of a university agriculture department, and determined to use science to help local farmers. **Nitrogen**, a substance found in soil, was the key.

Nitrogen

Nitrogen

Nitrogen

Cotton plants need a lot of nitrogen to grow, **stripping** it from the soil.

But other crops such as **peanuts**, actually **put** nitrogen **back** into the soil.

CROP ROTATION

So, planting cotton one year, then peanuts the next, kept nitrogen in the soil topped up. This was a known technique called **crop rotation**, but unlike other scientists, Carver took time to explain it to local farmers, which transformed their lives. He also researched over 400 different uses for peanuts.

Gradually, Carver became a scientific **celebrity**, winning prizes and advising three US Presidents.

FROM A GLOWING WIRE TO A
A LIGHTBULB MOMENT

In 1800, Alessandro Volta (see page 39) made a wire **glow** by passing electricity through it. This proved that **electricity** could make **light**. The race was now on to create a practical, long-lasting device to convert electricity into light — what was later to become known as an **incandescent lamp** or **lightbulb**. Many scientists tried, but the most successful was American inventor **Thomas Edison**.

THE PROBLEM...

Edison knew that, for safety, he needed to keep everything sealed inside a glass container. So what he needed now was a strip of something that could **glow** white-hot without **burning up** or **breaking**.

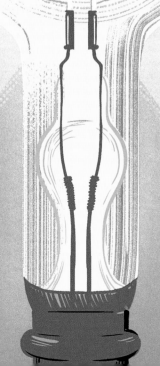

...SOLVED

After initial success with specially treated wood, paper, linen and cotton, Edison found that treated bamboo could **glow** for over a **thousand** hours. This made his design more practical than many others.

> I invented other things too, but perhaps my greatest contribution to science was setting up the world's first big **research laboratory**, where I employed many scientists to invent things for me.

DISCOVERING
HOW WE SEE

Ancient scientists believed our **eyes** emitted rays of light, and that was what allowed us to **see**. But, in the 10th century, a mathematician named **Ibn al-Haytham** proved this theory wrong...

Al-Haytham used a **dark room** with a hole in one side – an **albeit almuzlim** in Arabic, or **camera obscura** in Latin. When an object was placed in front of the hole, its upside-down image was cast onto the opposite wall. From this, he realized that light coming through the hole must travel in **straight lines**.

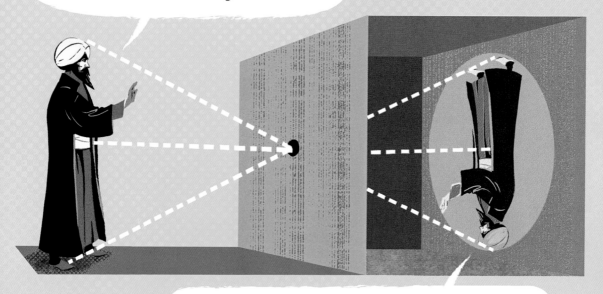

Through my experiments I proved that our eyes work in a similar way to my dark room. We see when rays of light bounce off objects and **enter our eyes**.

I studied ancient Greek descriptions of eyes. I also cut up bulls' eyes to learn as much as I could about their structure, and how they work.

Al-Haytham wrote down his findings in his **Book of Optics**, which contains a detailed drawing of the eyes and **optic nerves** – paths that send messages from the eyes to the brain. He also drew the oldest known illustration of the **nervous system**, which carries messages between the brain and the rest of the body.

HOW A SCIENTIST MADE
THE DESERT GREEN

In the 1970s, many scientists were worried that **deserts** were spreading over parts of Africa that once used to be green. They knew the answer was to **replant** millions of trees, but they weren't sure how to organize this, or pay for it. Then Kenyan biologist **Wangari Maathai** stepped in...

KENYA, 1970s

Developers **cut down** too many **trees**, leaving the soil bare.

Bare soil turned to **desert**.

This was bad for **wildlife** and for local **people** — they lost food, building materials and firewood.

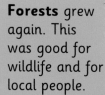

Forests grew again. This was good for wildlife and for local people.

Maathai organized thousands of volunteers to gather wild tree **seeds**.

They **grew** the seeds at home in re-used containers, then **planted** them in damaged areas.

My idea was such a success it **spread** around the world, and became known as the **Green Belt Movement**. In 2004 I was awarded a **Nobel Prize** for peace.

DISSECTING THE DEAD
TO UNDERSTAND THE LIVING

Until around 1500, not many scientists had **dissected** (cut up) dead people's bodies to find out exactly how they worked, or made accurate records of their findings. As a result, knowledge about the human body was often incomplete and inaccurate. But one scientist changed all that...

A NEW APPROACH

As a medical student in the 1530s, **Andreas Vesalius** first became fascinated by the human body. When he graduated, he took a job at the University of Padua, in Italy, specializing in **surgery** (operating on living patients) and **anatomy**, or the structure of the human body.

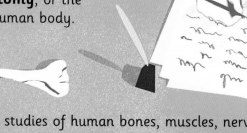

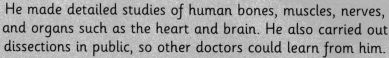

He made detailed studies of human bones, muscles, nerves, and organs such as the heart and brain. He also carried out dissections in public, so other doctors could learn from him.

Vesalius put all his knowledge in a huge book, **_On the Structure of the Human Body_**. He worked with artists to fill it with accurate drawings to back up his text, and invited readers to check his results for themselves.

A REVOLUTIONARY TEXTBOOK

His book was published in 1543. It **overturned** many **inaccurate ideas** that scientists had held for centuries, and had a **powerful influence** on scientists and doctors for centuries after.

HOW A SCIENTIST DISCOVERED
A NEW TYPE OF SHAPE

In the 1960s, mathematician **Benoit Mandelbrot** came across a seemingly simple question – how long is the coastline of Britain? He discovered that the answer wasn't simple because the closer you look at a coastline, the more bends and kinks you have to measure around, so the total length gets longer and longer. This led to a lifetime study of **shapes** that, like coastlines, **become more complex** the closer you look at them.

SHAPES IN NATURE

Mandelbrot started studying other shapes that had similar properties to coastlines, such as trees, ocean waves and snowflakes. As he zoomed in on these shapes, he found smaller and smaller versions of the original shape.

A NAME

Mandelbrot devised the name **fractals** for shapes like these.

This is a fractal shape known as the **Mandelbrot set**.

NEXT STEPS

Mandelbrot came up with a formula that described the mathematics behind fractals. He fed it into his computer. It created intriguing images, but most scientists dismissed them.

After years of patient work, Mandelbrot persuaded other scientists that the mathematics behind fractals is as **complex** and **interesting** as the shapes themselves. It's now used by scientists as diverse as geologists, medical researchers, astronomers and engineers.

THE MAN WHO
MEASURED THE WORLD

In ancient times, no one knew how big the Earth was, but a scientist living in Egypt, named **Eratosthenes**, found a way to calculate the planet's **circumference** (the distance around its middle) using just a few **simple measurements**.

EGYPT, AROUND 2,250 YEARS AGO...

Eratosthenes noticed that, at midday, buildings of the **same height** cast **shadows** of **different lengths** in different cities. He measured the **lengths** and **angles** of the two shadows.

Taking these measurements and the **distance** between the two cities, he was able to estimate the Earth's circumference with extraordinary accuracy.

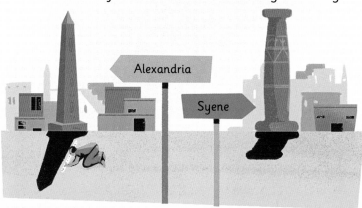

Alexandria

Syene

Eratosthenes' achievements didn't end there. He is thought to have invented **geography** – the study of the Earth, and created the first **map** known to include accurate distances between important places.

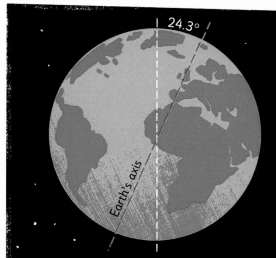

24.3°

Earth's axis

WATCHING THE STARS...

Eratosthenes saw how the stars seemed to **rotate** around the Earth. He concluded that it wasn't the stars that were spinning, but the Earth that must spin on an **axis** – an imaginary line that goes through its **middle**.

He also realized that this axis must be **tilted** at an angle, and he even made an accurate measurement of the tilt.

THE SCIENTISTS WHO WROTE THE RULES
BEHIND THE INTERNET

The internet is so widely used today that it's easy to take it for granted. But it took some very clever thinking to determine how large numbers of computers, with no one in overall control of them, could **send** and **receive** information in an orderly way. It was only after rules were in place that the **internet** became possible.

AMERICA, 1963

Computer scientists discussed the idea of linking up computers so information could be shared between them.

JOINING UP

By 1967, work had begun on the **ARPANET**, a small **network** of computers funded by the American military. By 1970, the network connected computers on the West and East coasts of America, but it was still seen as an obscure experiment.

REACHING OUT...

In 1972, American computer scientist **Bob Kahn** showed other computer experts how the ARPANET worked by connecting 20 computers. People suddenly realized the possibilities, but more work was needed.

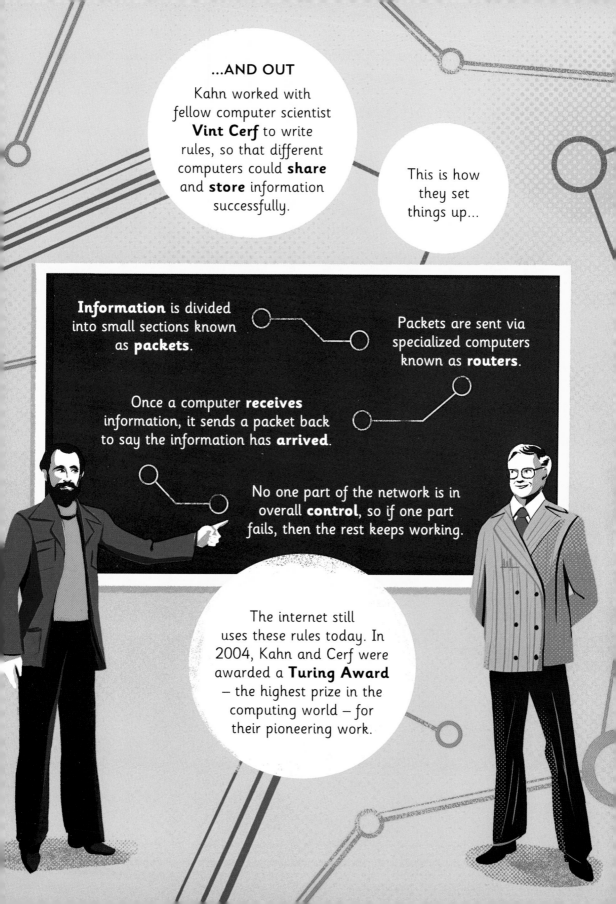

...AND OUT

Kahn worked with fellow computer scientist **Vint Cerf** to write rules, so that different computers could **share** and **store** information successfully.

This is how they set things up...

Information is divided into small sections known as **packets**.

Packets are sent via specialized computers known as **routers**.

Once a computer **receives** information, it sends a packet back to say the information has **arrived**.

No one part of the network is in overall **control**, so if one part fails, then the rest keeps working.

The internet still uses these rules today. In 2004, Kahn and Cerf were awarded a **Turing Award** – the highest prize in the computing world – for their pioneering work.

CALCULATING THE FATES
OF THE STARS

In 1930 a young Indian astrophysicist, **Subrahmanyan Chandrasekhar** (known as Chandra), made an important mathematical calculation. His workings ultimately explained the existence of two of the most mysterious things in the universe – **neutron stars** and **black holes**.

SIZE MATTERS

Stars burn brightly for millions of years, but eventually they begin to cool and die. Chandra proved that they go through different stages, depending on their **size**.

When a **medium-sized** star around the size of our Sun begins to die, it becomes a **white dwarf** – a small, cold, incredibly dense sphere that shines a brilliant white before burning out.

His calculations showed that a **larger** star (around four to eight times as massive as our Sun) does not become a white dwarf...

...instead, it collapses, becoming a very compact and heavy type of star called a **neutron star**.

Chandra used his results to show that an even bigger star – 20 or more times as massive as our Sun – collapses to a point where gravity is so strong that **nothing** can escape it, not even light. This is a **black hole**.

HELPING SAILORS
AND SCIENTISTS FIND THEIR WAY

In ancient times, very few women were allowed to pursue an education. Despite this, nearly 2,000 years ago, one of the most highly respected scholars in the city of Alexandria, Egypt, was a woman named **Hypatia**. She made significant contributions to **philosophy**, **astronomy**, **mathematics** and more...

READING THE STARS

Hypatia was skilled at constructing **plane astrolabes** – tools used to measure the positions of the stars and planets, which helped sailors to find their way at sea.

Plane astrolabe

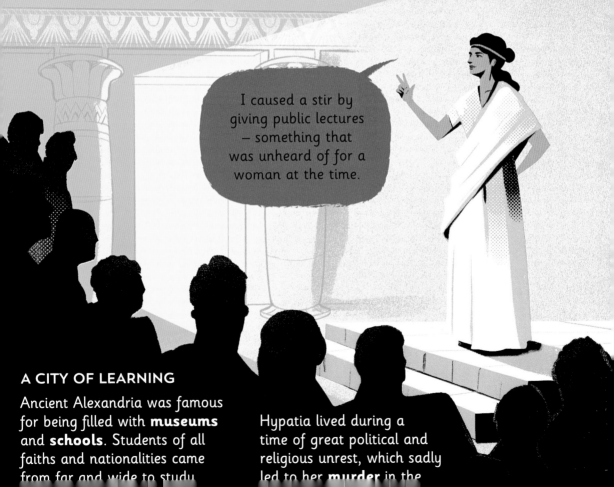

I caused a stir by giving public lectures – something that was unheard of for a woman at the time.

A CITY OF LEARNING

Ancient Alexandria was famous for being filled with **museums** and **schools**. Students of all faiths and nationalities came from far and wide to study.

Hypatia lived during a time of great political and religious unrest, which sadly led to her **murder** in the

THE 18TH-CENTURY GUIDE TO
ORDERING THE NATURAL WORLD

To identify living things and see how they are related, modern scientists use a system of **classification** that developed out of the work of Swedish botanist **Carl Linnaeus**. He started with three giant groups: **animal**, **vegetable** and **mineral**. He then split these into smaller and smaller categories.

This example shows how a **black bear** fits into Linnaeus's categories for animals. The modern system uses even more categories.

KINGDOM: ANIMAL

This huge group (called a **kingdom**) includes **all** animals — from tiny bugs and slugs to birds, sea creatures and **black bears**.

CLASS: MAMMAL

The animal kingdom is divided into groups known as **classes**. One of these is a group that feeds its young with milk — **mammals**. This includes bats, dolphins, kangaroos and **black bears**.

ORDER: CARNIVORE

Some mammals, including **black bears**, tigers and meerkats, are in a group (or **order**) known as carnivores — **meat-eaters**.

GENUS: BEAR

Bears is a group (called a **genus**) within meat-eating mammals. It includes **black bears**, panda bears, brown bears and others.

Here you can see that black bears are most closely related to other bears, and are more distantly related to other meat-eating mammals.

SPECIES: BLACK BEAR

This smaller group, or **species**, within bears only includes **black bears**.

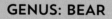

FROM SPINNING GALAXIES
TO DARK MATTER

The **Universe** still holds many mysteries. But thanks to one astronomer's meticulous observations, we are a little closer to understanding one of them...

AMERICA, LATE 1970s

Astronomer **Vera Rubin** was studying the **spiral-shaped** Andromeda Galaxy as it rotated in space. She expected the stars on the outside to be moving much more slowly than those near the middle. But in fact all the stars were moving at **exactly the same speed**.

She studied over sixty spiral galaxies, and found the **same thing** every time. The stars' rotation speed meant the whole galaxy should have **flown apart**, so why hadn't this happened?

Rubin soon connected her findings to other scientists' theories about **dark matter** — a substance whose presence can only be detected from the effect it has on **other** things such as stars and galaxies.

Rubin concluded that it must be dark matter that was **holding together** the stars in galaxies. Most scientists at the time didn't believe dark matter existed, but Rubin's results could not be ignored.

Now, 40 years after Rubin's discovery, dark matter is thought to make up about around **85% of the Universe**. But what it is actually made from still remains a mystery

HOW CREATING LIFE IN A LABORATORY
GAVE HOPE TO MILLIONS

Most women become pregnant when an egg from one of their ovaries is **fertilized**. But for some women this isn't possible. In the 1960s, **three dedicated scientists** developed a procedure that gave hope to women struggling to conceive.

BRITAIN, 1960s

A doctor named **Robert Edwards** was convinced it was possible to **remove** an egg from an ovary, and fertilize it in a laboratory. The only problem was he didn't know how to perform this operation.

Meanwhile, surgeon **Patrick Steptoe** was pioneering the use of a piece of equipment called a **laparoscope**. This was a thin telescopic tube with a tiny camera and light, that could be inserted though a patient's abdomen to **diagnose** fertility problems.

Steptoe wondered if a laparoscope could also be used to help **treat** fertility problems.

TEAMWORK

In 1966, Edwards and Steptoe teamed up. Using a laparoscope, they removed eggs and fertilized them in glass dishes. A fertilized egg could then be replanted in the mother. This procedure became known as **in vitro fertilization**, or **IVF**. *In vitro* means "in glass" in Latin.

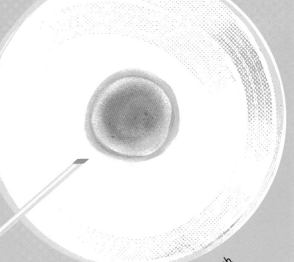

Eggs are fertilized in a dish

In 1968, nurse **Jean Purdy** joined Edwards and Steptoe as a laboratory technician, to assist with **IVF treatments**.

Fertilized eggs

Purdy quickly became an indispensable part of the team, helping Edwards on over a hundred IVF procedures. None of them resulted in a **lasting pregnancy**, until...

SUCCESS!

A new patient came along, Lesley Brown, who had been trying to have a child for 15 years. This time, the pregnancy lasted. On July 25, 1978, Lesley gave birth to the **world's first IVF baby** – Louise Brown.

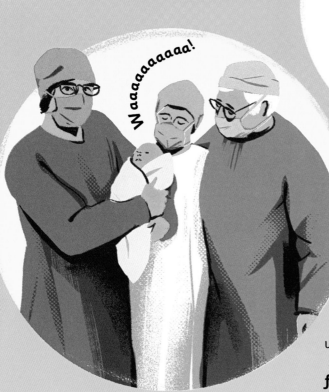

Waaaaaaaaaa!

A NEW GENERATION

Louise's birth gave hope to thousands of people previously unable to have a child. Edwards, Steptoe and Purdy founded the **first ever fertility clinic**. Since then, around the world, over **8 million** children have been born as a result of IVF treatment.

HOW BLOSSOM THE COW
HELPED WIPE OUT A DEADLY DISEASE

During the **18th century**, the world was ravaged by a deadly disease called **smallpox**. One doctor found a cure and saved millions of lives — all thanks to a cow named **Blossom**.

BRITAIN, 1773

A country doctor named **Edward Jenner** had a visit from a local milkmaid. She had scabs on her arm, and was scared that she had caught **smallpox**.

Do I have it, Dr. Jenner?

In fact, she had **cowpox**, a less serious infection caught from her cow, **Blossom**.

JENNER WAS INTRIGUED...

A **local legend** claimed that smallpox never affected milkmaids. Did cowpox **protect** humans against smallpox?

Jenner took a sample of cowpox from one of the milkmaid's scabs, and used it to infect a local boy. The boy became unwell, but **recovered**.

Two months later, Jenner infected the boy with smallpox. The smallpox **didn't affect him at all**.

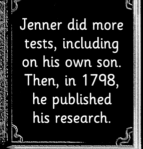

Jenner did more tests, including on his own son. Then, in 1798, he published his research.

News of the cure spread around the world. It became known as a **vaccine**, from *vacca* — "cow" in Latin. Jenner dedicated the rest of his life to teaching people how to **vaccinate** against smallpox.

ALL CLEAR

In 1979, the World Health Organization finally declared smallpox **eradicated**.

EXPLORING
THE DEEP

Before the late 1800s, scientists thought that life could only exist in the parts of the ocean where there was **sunlight**. A British marine biologist named **Charles Wyville Thomson** helped prove this wasn't true...

I heard reports from Norwegian biologist Michael Sars that he had caught fish in **very deep** nets.

1868 & 1869

Thomson dragged his own nets through the **Atlantic Ocean.** He found fish, corals, sponges, starfish, and more, thriving in places so deep that **no light** ever reached them.

Later, he went on a voyage, exploring the Atlantic, Pacific and Indian oceans. He and his team discovered over **4,000** previously unknown species, proving that deep-sea life can and does exist in oceans **all over the world**.

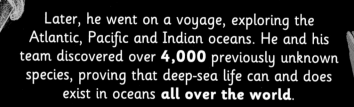

HOW AN OCTOPUS
HELPED SET THE RULES OF SCIENCE

In ancient times, there weren't any **rules** for scientists, so they had to decide for themselves what was and what wasn't a **scientific fact**. Many of their ideas were based on **traditions**, **legends** or **stories** that weren't scientifically accurate. But that began to change in Greece around 2,300 years ago...

OBSERVING CAREFULLY

An ancient Greek scientist and thinker named **Aristotle** realized that the only accurate way to learn about the world was by **looking** at it (or hearing, touching, tasting or smelling it) very **carefully**.

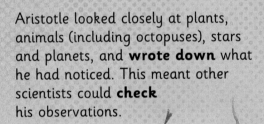

Aristotle looked closely at plants, animals (including octopuses), stars and planets, and **wrote down** what he had noticed. This meant other scientists could **check** his observations.

ADDING EXPERIMENTS...

Later scientists, such as Al-Haytham (see page 83), followed Aristotle's example. But this time they also **measured** things (to compare them accurately with other things) and did **experiments**, to test how things behaved.

AND MATHEMATICS...

Italian scientist Galileo (see page 26) measured, did experiments and made observations and notes. He also used **mathematics**, instead of words, to write down some of his observations.

THE SCIENTIFIC METHOD

All these techniques are now part of **the scientific method** – a set of rules for scientists. This helps scientists compare their results and agree about what is and isn't a scientific fact.

INVESTIGATING HOW WE ARE
BORN MALE OR FEMALE

It wasn't until just over a hundred years ago that a scientist first discovered what it was that caused animals or people to be born **male** or **female**. The answer lay inside **cells** — the minute building blocks living things are made from — in structures now known as **chromosomes**.

AMERICA, 1905

Biologist **Nettie Stevens** was studying butterflies, fruit flies and beetles. She looked at the cells they use for **reproduction**.

In the cells of the **female** bugs, she saw two **X-shaped chromosomes**. The **male** bugs had one X-shaped chromosome and one **Y-shaped** one.

Stevens realized that...

the **mother** passes an **X** chromosome to each baby.

the **father** can pass on either an **X** or a **Y**.

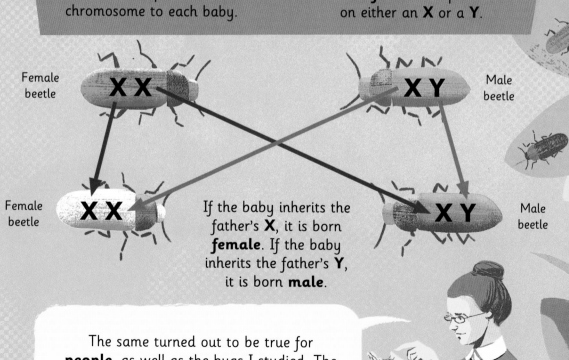

Female beetle **X X**

Male beetle **X Y**

Female beetle **X X**

If the baby inherits the father's **X**, it is born **female**. If the baby inherits the father's **Y**, it is born **male**.

Male beetle **X Y**

The same turned out to be true for **people**, as well as the bugs I studied. The **father's chromosomes** are what **decide** whether a baby is born **male** or **female**.

TAKING ILLNESS OUT OF
THE HANDS OF THE GODS

Around 2,400 years ago in Ancient Greece, most people believed that sickness was caused by **evil spirits** or **angry gods**. One doctor, known as **Hippocrates**, thought differently...

Hippocrates set up a medical school on the Greek island of Kos, where he became fascinated by the causes and treatment of **diseases**.

By closely observing patients, he grew convinced that illnesses had **natural causes**.

I was the **first doctor** to **diagnose** heart and lung diseases, and to suggest that thoughts occur in the brain, rather than the heart.

Hippocrates also taught doctors new ways to behave towards patients, such as keeping their information **confidential**.

FROM ANCIENT TO MODERN

Today, new doctors promise to uphold a series of **ethical rules** of their profession, based on his teachings. This is known as

THE HUMAN COMPUTER
WHO SENT PEOPLE TO THE MOON

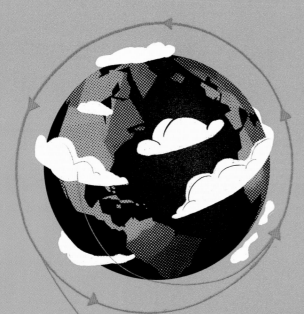

In the early days of **space flight**, space agencies relied on **people**, not **computers**, to make the incredibly **complex calculations** needed to find the angle a spacecraft should fly at, the route it should take, and the time it should take off. One outstanding mathematician led the way...

AMERICA, 1953

African-American mathematician **Katherine Johnson** worked at the National Advisory Committee for Aeronautics, or **NACA**. She was one of a team, known as **human computers**, who made all the calculations for aircraft flights.

SPACE FLIGHT

In 1958, NACA became **NASA**, the American space agency. Johnson now worked on calculations for space flights. NASA started using electronic computers in 1962, but Johnson was asked to check their accuracy.

In 1969, NASA landed the first ever people on the Moon. Johnson's calculations were crucial to the mission's success.

In 2015 Johnson was awarded the **Presidential Medal of Freedom**, America's highest non-military award.

THE SCIENTIST WHO INVENTED
GEOLOGY

Before the late 1700s, people believed the face of the Earth had remained **unchanged** since the dawn of time. But one scientist realized that **natural forces** are constantly (but very, very slowly) **destroying** old rocks and **making** new ones.

SCOTLAND, 1760S

Farmer and naturalist **James Hutton** studied rocks and how they were formed. He came up with the idea that they are constantly being **recycled**.

HOW IT WORKS...

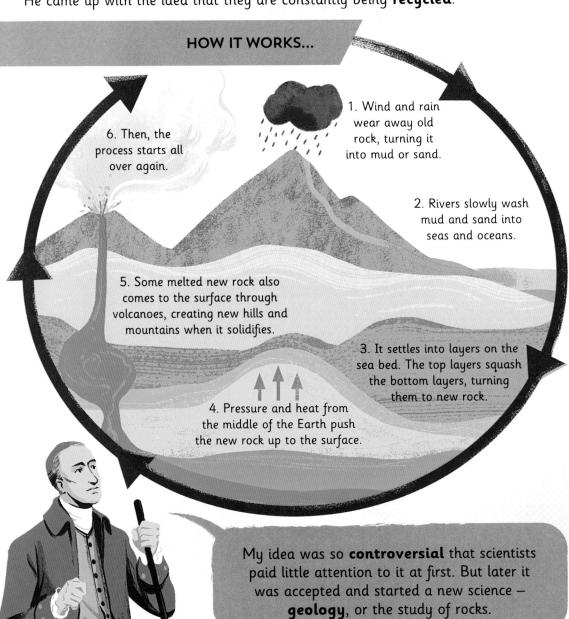

6. Then, the process starts all over again.

1. Wind and rain wear away old rock, turning it into mud or sand.

2. Rivers slowly wash mud and sand into seas and oceans.

5. Some melted new rock also comes to the surface through volcanoes, creating new hills and mountains when it solidifies.

3. It settles into layers on the sea bed. The top layers squash the bottom layers, turning them to new rock.

4. Pressure and heat from the middle of the Earth push the new rock up to the surface.

My idea was so **controversial** that scientists paid little attention to it at first. But later it was accepted and started a new science — **geology**, or the study of rocks.

SOLVING THE PUZZLE OF
THE CONTINENTS

For a long time, no one knew why the outlines of Earth's **continents** look the way they do. I noticed that they seemed almost like pieces of a **jigsaw puzzle**, and formed a theory to explain why...

220 million years ago

GERMANY, 1912

Polar explorer and meteorologist **Alfred Wegener** proposed that all the continents had once been joined together in a **supercontinent**. Over millions of years, he suggested, this had come apart, creating separate continents that **drifted** away from each other.

135 million years ago

Wegener found similarities in **rocks and fossils** across different continents, and suggested this was proof that they were once joined together. But his theory — known as **continental drift** — couldn't explain **how** the continents had moved so far apart.

Today

MOVING PLATES

From the 1950s, scientists began to find the answer: Earth's crust is made of **plates**, which are constantly moving. The science of studying Earth's crust is called **plate tectonics** — and it all began with Wegener's theory.

GETTING TO THE HEART OF
CIRCULATION

For centuries, scientists puzzled over how **blood circulates** through the **heart**. Two doctors, working three hundred years apart, set out to solve this mystery...

EGYPT, 13TH CENTURY...

A Syrian doctor named **Ibn al-Nafis** believed that the ancient textbooks most doctors at that time depended on weren't as reliable as careful observation.

Through his investigations, he was the first person to find out how the **heart** and **lungs** work together.

Blood flows from the **right** side of the heart to the lungs, where it picks up **air**. Then it flows to the **left** side of the heart, before **circulating** around the body.

From the upper body

THE HEART

Blood from the lungs to the left side of the heart

Blood enters the **right side of the heart**, and is pumped...

...to the lungs to pick up oxygen.

This diagram shows how blood flows through the heart

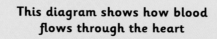

Blood filled with **oxygen**

Blood with **less oxygen**

Blood from the lower body

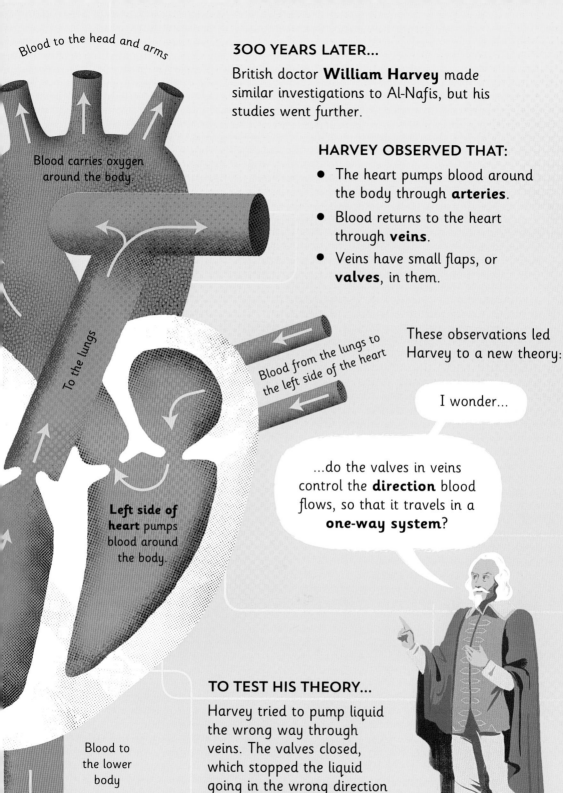

Blood to the head and arms

Blood carries oxygen around the body.

To the lungs

Left side of heart pumps blood around the body.

Blood from the lungs to the left side of the heart

Blood to the lower body

300 YEARS LATER...

British doctor **William Harvey** made similar investigations to Al-Nafis, but his studies went further.

HARVEY OBSERVED THAT:

- The heart pumps blood around the body through **arteries**.
- Blood returns to the heart through **veins**.
- Veins have small flaps, or **valves**, in them.

These observations led Harvey to a new theory:

I wonder...

...do the valves in veins control the **direction** blood flows, so that it travels in a **one-way system**?

TO TEST HIS THEORY...

Harvey tried to pump liquid the wrong way through veins. The valves closed, which stopped the liquid going in the wrong direction – just as he had thought.

TEACHING COMPUTERS
TO SPEAK ENGLISH

Early computers needed trained mathematicians who could write **mathematical instructions** to tell them what to do. This is known as **programming**. In the 1950s, one of these mathematicians, **Grace Hopper**, decided to make programming easier. She created the first system that used **words** instead of numbers and symbols.

When Hopper first told computer experts she could develop a system of programming using words, they didn't believe her. But she went ahead anyway.

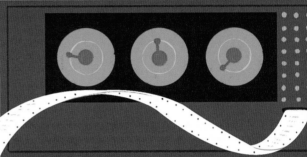

By 1959 she had developed **FLOW-MATIC**. It let programmers type instructions for a particular brand of computer using words. The computer then **translated** the words into mathematical **codes**.

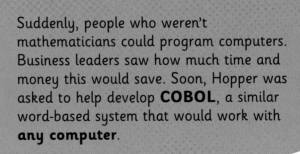

Suddenly, people who weren't mathematicians could program computers. Business leaders saw how much time and money this would save. Soon, Hopper was asked to help develop **COBOL**, a similar word-based system that would work with **any computer**.

COBOL was incredibly popular, and it is still in use. Today, new technology allows people to **speak** to their computers. But it was Grace Hopper who took the first step in this direction, by proving that computers could understand words.

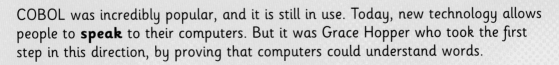

MAKING DISCOVERIES ABOUT
SPACE AND TIME

In the early 1650s, Dutch physicist **Christiaan Huygens** built an incredibly powerful telescope, and made astonishing discoveries about the Solar System...

Huygens observed that **Saturn** was circled by **rings**.

He also discovered Saturn's largest moon, now called **Titan**.

He studied and sketched an area of stars and gas called the **Orion Nebula**...

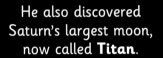

...and was the first person to observe a surface feature on another planet – a volcanic plain on **Mars**.

KEEPING TIME

Astronomers needed to keep time carefully, to track stars. Huygens designed a clock that used the swinging motion of a **pendulum** to measure time. It was the most accurate timekeeper that had ever been built.

A NEW WAVE THEORY

In 1678, Huygens proposed that light moved in **waves**. Few scientists agreed, but this theory was later proved to be correct, and helped explain how light rays can bend.

HOW A MESSY LAB
SAVED MILLIONS OF LIVES

The world's first antibiotic was discovered by accident, when a British scientist found an unknown fungus growing in a corner of a his untidy lab...

LONDON, 1928
Alexander Fleming was growing **bacteria** in his lab. One day, he returned from a month's break...

That's funny! A **strange fungus** has grown on one of my dishes.

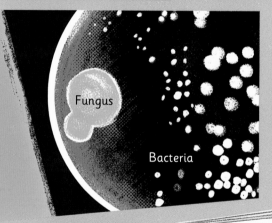

Fleming looked closer. Bacteria near the fungus had been **killed**, while those further away were **still alive**.

Fungus

Bacteria

He extracted a chemical from the fungus and named it **penicillin**. But he had trouble producing penicillin in big enough quantities to treat patients.

IN THE 1940s
Working separately, two other scientists – Howard Florey and Ernst Boris Chain – developed a way to **mass-produce** penicillin to treat **serious infections** caused by bacteria.

NOBEL PRIZE AWARDED

In 1945 the three scientists shared a **Nobel Prize**. By then, penicillin had saved **millions of lives**.

MORE INFORMATION

On the following pages, you'll find a timeline of the lives of the 100 scientists whose discoveries are described in this book. There's also a glossary explaining the scientific terms used.

TIMELINE

ERATOSTHENES
276-194 BCE
Greek scientist working in Alexandria, Egypt, who was the first to measure the **Earth's circumference** accurately.

HIPPOCRATES
c.460-370 BCE
Greek doctor who was the first known to **diagnose diseases** of the heart and lungs.

ARISTOTLE
384-322 BCE
Greek thinker who devised a **scientific method** of study based on close observation of nature.

HYPATIA OF ALEXANDRIA
c.360-415
A Greek astronomer, mathematician and **influential teacher** who worked in Alexandria.

The letter c. before a date means the precise date isn't known. Dates with the letters BC or BCE are from the time *Before Christ* was born, or *Before the Common Era*. They are counted back from the year 1.

GOTTFRIED LEIBNIZ
1646-1716
German mathematician who (separately from Newton) invented **calculus**.

To every action there is always opposed an equal reaction.

CHRISTIAAN HUYGENS
1629-1695
Dutch physicist, astronomer and inventor who designed the first **pendulum clock**.

ISAAC NEWTON
1643-1727
British physicist, astronomer and mathematician who discovered the **laws of motion** and **gravity**.

ROBERT HOOKE
1635-1703
British scientist who pioneered the use of **microscopes** and first named **cells** – the building blocks that make up living things.

MARIA SYBILLA MERIAN
1647-1717
German artist and naturalist who published influential books on **insect life cycles**.

JAMES HUTTON
1726-1797
British farmer and naturalist, whose work studying how rocks are formed became the basis of modern **geology**.

CARL LINNAEUS
1707-1778
Swedish botanist who developed **classification** – organizing living things into categories.

WILLIAM HERSCHEL
1738-1822
German-British astronomer to British King George III; discovered the planet **Uranus**.

MUHAMMAD IBN MUSA AL-KHWARIZMI
C.780-C.850
Persian mathematician (working in what are now Iran and Iraq) who invented **algebra**.

IBN SINA
980-1037
Doctor born in what is now Uzbekistan. His **medical textbook** was used by doctors throughout the Middle East and Europe.

BRAHMAGUPTA
598-668
Indian mathematician, the first person to write down rules for using **zero** and numbers smaller than zero.

IBN AL-HAYTHAM
965-1040
Arab scientist who studied **optics** – how light works – and how we see.

SHEN KUO
1031-1095
Chinese government official who wrote *Dream Pool Essays* – a collection of his scientific discoveries.

GALILEO GALILEI
1564-1642
Italian astronomer who discovered three of Jupiter's moons, and **proved Copernicus's theory** that the Earth orbits the Sun.

IBN AL-NAFIS
1213-1288
Syrian doctor who was the first to describe accurately how **blood circulates** through the heart and lungs.

WILLIAM HARVEY
1578-1657
British doctor who described how **blood circulates** around the body.

ANDREAS VESALIUS
1514-1564
A doctor from Brussels who published one of the most influential books on **human anatomy**.

NICOLAUS COPERNICUS
1473-1543
Polish astronomer who proposed the idea that the **Earth travels around the Sun**.

ANTOINE LAVOISIER
1743-1794
French chemist who identified and named the element **oxygen**.

In nature nothing is created, nothing is lost, everything changes.

EDWARD JENNER
1749-1823
British doctor who discovered the **vaccine** against smallpox.

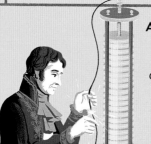

ALESSANDRO VOLTA
1745-1827
Italian physicist and chemist who created the world's first **battery**.

CAROLINE HERSCHEL
1750-1848
German-British astronomer who became Britain's **first paid professional** woman scientist.

ALEXANDER VON HUMBOLDT
1769-1859
German naturalist and explorer who was the first to describe **climate change** caused by human activity.

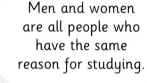

Men and women are all people who have the same reason for studying.

WANG ZHENYI
1768-1797
Chinese astronomer who found out what causes **lunar eclipses**.

GEORGES CUVIER
1769-1832
French zoologist who was the first to prove that animal species could become **extinct**.

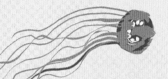

WILHELM RÖNTGEN
1845-1923
German physicist who discovered **X-rays**.

DMITRI MENDELEEV
1834-1907
Russian chemist who created the **Periodic Table** of chemical elements still used today.

CHARLES WYVILLE THOMSON
1830-1882
British marine biologist; the first to prove that **deep-sea creatures** exist.

ROBERT KOCH
1843-1910
German doctor and microbiologist who found the **bacteria** that cause tuberculosis, anthrax and cholera.

JAMES CLERK MAXWELL
1831-1879
British physicist who showed that magnetism, light and electricity are all forms of **electromagnetic waves**.

ALEXANDER GRAHAM BELL
1847-1922
Scottish-born inventor based in Canada and the US, who **invented** the **telephone**.

GEORGE WASHINGTON CARVER
1864-1943
American agricultural scientist who promoted **farming methods** to improve soil quality.

THOMAS EDISON
1847-1931
American inventor of the **lightbulb** who set up the first industrial science laboratory.

SVANTE ARRHENIUS
1859-1927
Swedish scientist who worked on acids and bases, and predicted **global warming**.

NETTIE STEVENS
1861-1912
American geneticist who discovered **sex chromosomes**.

RICHARD TREVITHICK
1771-1833
British engineer who designed the first **steam-powered locomotive**.

CHARLES BABBAGE
1791-1871
British mathematician who designed, but never built, the world's **first computer**.

MICHAEL FARADAY
1791-1867
British scientist whose experiments in **electricity** created the first **generator**.

MARY ANNING
1799-1847
British fossil collector who discovered many **prehistoric creatures**.

CHARLES DARWIN
1809-1882
British naturalist who came up with the theory of **evolution by natural selection**.

LOUIS PASTEUR
1822-1895
French chemist and microbiologist who proved that **germs** can cause food to go bad and cause diseases.

The love for all living creatures is the most noble attribute of man.

GREGOR MENDEL
1822-1884
Austrian monk whose work with pea plants formed the basis of **genetics**.

ADA LOVELACE
1815-1852
British mathematician who wrote the first ever **computer program**.

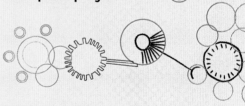

Be less curious about people and more curious about ideas.

WILBUR WRIGHT
1867-1912
American pioneer of **powered flight**.

KARL LANDSTEINER
1868-1943
Austrian doctor who discovered the main **blood groups**.

MARIE CURIE
1867-1934
Polish-French scientist who studied **radioactivity**, and discovered two radioactive elements.

YNES MEXIA
1870-1938
Mexican-American botanist known for her huge collection of **plant specimens**.

ERNEST RUTHERFORD
1871-1937
New Zealand physicist who came to be known as the father of **nuclear physics**.

GUGLIELMO MARCONI
1874-1937
Italian scientist known for his pioneering work on long-distance **radio transmission**.

ORVILLE WRIGHT
1871-1948
American pioneer of **powered flight**.

LISE MEITNER
1878-1968
Austrian-Swedish physicist who worked on **radioactivity** and **nuclear physics**.

BARBARA MCCLINTOCK
1902-1992
American geneticist who discovered that **genes** can jump around.

It is no good to try to stop knowledge from going forward.

SATYENDRA NATH BOSE
1894-1974
Indian physicist who, along with Albert Einstein, theorized that particles later called **bosons** existed.

PAUL DIRAC
1902-1984
British physicist who made fundamental contributions to early **quantum field theory**.

ENRICO FERMI
1901-1954
Italian-American physicist who created the world's first **nuclear reactor**.

CECILIA PAYNE-GAPOSCHKIN
1900-1979
British-American astronomer who discovered that stars are made primarily of **hydrogen** and **helium**.

TOMMY FLOWERS
1905-1998
British engineer who designed and built the world's first **programmable electronic computer**.

RACHEL CARSON
1907-1964
American scientist whose writings advanced the **environmental** movement.

The aim of science is to discover and illuminate the truth.

GRACE HOPPER
1906-1992
American computer scientist and US navy admiral. Pioneer of **computer programming**.

> Science can flourish only in an atmosphere of free speech.

ALFRED WEGENER
1880-1930
German polar researcher and geophysicist who developed the theory of **continental drift**.

ALEXANDER FLEMING
1881-1955
British biologist who discovered **penicillin**.

ALBERT EINSTEIN
1879-1955
German-American theoretical physicist who changed the way we understand things such as **light, gravity and time**.

ERNEST EVERETT JUST
1883-1941
American biologist who discovered that **cells** can behave differently in a lab than in their natural conditions.

EDWIN HUBBLE
1889-1953
American astronomer whose research helped prove that the Universe is **expanding**.

SRINIVASA RAMANUJAN
1887-1920
Self-taught Indian mathematician who had a **number** named after him.

INGE LEHMANN
1888-1993
Danish seismologist who discovered that the Earth has a **solid inner core**.

NIELS BOHR
1885-1962
Danish physicist who contributed to the understanding of **atomic structure** and **quantum theory**.

SUBRAHMANYAN CHANDRASEKHAR
1910-1995
Indian-American astrophysicist whose calculations helped explain how **white dwarfs**, **neutron stars** and **black holes** are formed.

> Those who can imagine anything, can create the impossible.

LUIS ALVAREZ
1911-1988
American physicist who, along with Walter Alvarez, discovered the probable cause of the dinosaurs' **extinction**.

ALAN TURING
1912-1954
British mathematician and code-breaker. Often called the father of **modern computing**.

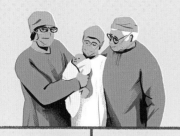

HISAKO KOYAMA
1916-1997
Japanese astronomer who dedicated her life to **observing the Sun**.

Everything is physics and math.

FRANCIS CRICK
1916-2004
British biologist who helped discover the structure of **DNA**.

PATRICK STEPTOE
1913-1988
British doctor who helped develop **IVF** treatment.

KATHERINE JOHNSON
1918-
American mathematician whose calculations were critical to the first **space flights**.

WANGARI MAATHAI
1940-2011
Kenyan environmentalist who founded the **Green Belt Movement**.

ROBERT WOODROW WILSON
1936-
American astronomer who helped discover **Cosmic Microwave Background radiation**.

JANE GOODALL
1934-
British primatologist and world's leading expert on **chimpanzees**.

WALTER ALVAREZ
1940-
American geologist, who, with his father Luis Alvarez, discovered the probable cause of the dinosaurs' **extinction**.

BOB KAHN
1938-
American computer scientist who helped make the **internet** a reality.

STEPHEN HAWKING
1942-2018
British physicist known for his work with **black holes** and **relativity**.

JEAN PURDY
1945-1985
British nurse who helped develop **IVF** treatment.

VINT CERF
1943-
American computer scientist who helped make the **internet** a reality.

SHUJI NAKAMURA
1954-
Japanese scientist who invented super-efficient blue and white **LEDs**.

Science and everyday life cannot and should not be separated.

BENOIT MANDELBROT
1924-2010
Polish-French-American mathematician who developed the field of **fractal geometry**.

GERTRUDE ELION
1918-1999
American biochemist who created a systematic method for **designing new drugs**.

ROSALIND FRANKLIN
1920-1958
British chemist who helped discover the structure of **DNA**.

ROBERT EDWARDS
1925-2013
British doctor who helped develop **IVF** treatment.

VERA RUBIN
1928-2016
American astronomer who discovered evidence of the existence of **dark matter**.

ARNO ALLAN PENZIAS
1933-
American astronomer who helped discover **Cosmic Microwave Background radiation**.

PETER HIGGS
1929-
British physicist known for his work on **subatomic** (smaller than atoms) **particles**.

TU YOUYOU
1930-
Chinese chemist who created the first effective modern treatment for **malaria**.

JAMES WATSON
1928-
American biologist who helped discover the structure of **DNA**.

SOOKYUNG CHOI
1957-
Korean physicist who discovered a new kind of particle called a **X(3872) meson**.

MAY-BRITT MOSER
1963-
Norwegian neuroscientist who discovered how the **brain** makes maps.

TIM BERNERS-LEE
1955-
British computer scientist and inventor of the **World Wide Web**.

LENE HAU
1959-
Danish physicist who first slowed, then stopped a **beam of light**.

GLOSSARY

This glossary explains some of the words used in this book.
Words shown in **bold** have their own entries.

ACID — A corrosive and sour-tasting substance. The opposite of a **base**.

ALGEBRA — A type of **mathematics** used to solve problems when some numbers are unknown.

ALGORITHM — A way of solving a mathematical or computer problem.

ANATOMY — The study of the structure of bodies and how they work.

ANTIBIOTIC — A type of **medicine**, such as penicillin, used to treat infections caused by **bacteria**.

ANTIMATTER — A type of matter, such as a **positron**.

ARTERY — A large blood vessel that carries blood away from the heart.

ASTRONOMY — The study of space.

ASTROPHYSICS — The study of the origin and nature of the **Universe**, including how stars work.

ATOMS — Incredibly tiny **particles**; the building blocks of all matter.

AXIS — A real or imaginary line through the middle of an object, around which it turns.

BACTERIA — **Microscopic** living things that can sometimes cause illness.

BASE — A corrosive substance. The opposite of an **acid**.

BIG BANG, THE — A massive explosion that is thought to have started the **Universe** from a single, tiny point.

BIOLOGY — The study of living things.

BLACK HOLE — A point in **spacetime** with such strong **gravity** that not even light can escape.

BLOOD TRANSFUSION — Putting the blood of one person into the bloodstream of another.

BOSON — A type of **subatomic** particle named after Satyendra Nath Bose.

BOTANY — The study of plants.

CALCULUS — A type of **mathematics** used for calculating things such as the area of a curved shape.

CARBON DIOXIDE — A gas made of carbon and oxygen, produced by burning fuels, and also breathed out by humans and animals.

CELL — The basic unit of living things.

CHEMISTRY — The study of **elements** and **compounds** — how they work, what they are made of, their structures, and how they react with other substances.

CHROMOSOMES — strings of **DNA** found inside **cells**.

CLIMATE CHANGE — Long-term changes to global weather conditions.

COMBUSTION — The act or process of burning.

COMET — An object in space made up of dust and ice that travels around the Sun.

COMPOUND — A substance made of different types of **atoms** bonded into **molecules**.

COMPUTER PROGRAM — A list of instructions that tells a computer what to do.

COMPUTER SCIENCE — The study of the workings and use of computers.

COSMIC MICROWAVE BACKGROUND — A type of **radiation** that can be detected throughout the **Universe**.

CURRENT — The flow of electricity, air or water.

DARK MATTER — A form of matter that cannot be detected, but we know exists because of its visible effect on other objects.

DNA — A twin spiral, ladder-shaped **molecule** that **genes** are made of. Short for deoxyribonucleic acid.

EARTHQUAKE — A movement of the Earth's surface.

ECOSYSTEM — A community where all the living things and their environment depend on one another.

ELECTROMAGNETISM — The interaction between electricity and magnetism; travels in waves.

ELECTROMAGNETIC RADIATION — **Radiation** made of electromagnetic waves, including radio waves, light and **X-rays**.

ELECTRON — A subatomic **particle** that moves around the **nucleus** of an **atom**.

ELEMENT — A substance made up of one type of **atom**, which cannot be broken down to form a simpler substance.

EVOLUTION — The way **species** of living things change over time.

EXTINCT — A **species** goes extinct, and no longer exists, when the last individual member of that species dies.

FERMION — A type of **subatomic particle** named after Enrico Fermi.

FORMULA — A rule or way of doing something, using words or symbols.

FORCE — A push or pull that changes the motion or shape of an object.

FOSSIL — The shape of a living thing or its remains preserved inside rock.

FRACTAL — A very irregular line or surface formed of an endless number of irregular sections.

GALAXY — A group of billions of stars that orbit around a central point.

GENE — A section of **DNA** that holds coded information.

GENETICS — The study of how **genes** affect living things.

GEOLOGY — The study of the Earth — especially rocks.

GERMS — **Microscopic** living things, such as **bacteria**, that cause illness or cause food and drinks to go bad.

GRAVITY — The **force** of two objects pulling on each other due to their **mass**.

HIGGS BOSON — A type of **boson** (a **subatomic particle**) that takes its name from Peter Higgs.

INTERNET — The global system of computer networks that lets computer users to connect to other users.

IT — Short for Information Technology — the study of systems used for storing and sharing information.

LASER — A beam of powerful light.

MAGNET — An object that has magnetic force — an invisible force that attracts other objects.

MAGNETIC FIELD — The area around a **magnet** in which objects are affected by the magnet's force.

MASS — A measure of how much of a substance is present and also its resistance to changes in motion.

MATHEMATICS —The study of numbers, amounts, shapes and the relationships between them.

MESON — A type of **subatomic** particle, usually made of a **quark** and an anti-quark.

METEORITE — A piece of rock from outer space that has landed on Earth.

MICROBE — **Microscopic** living things, such as **germs** and **bacteria**.

MICROSCOPIC — Anything too small to be seen without a microscope.

MILKY WAY — The **galaxy** that contains our **solar system**. Can be seen in the night sky as a long, cloudy group of stars.

MOLECULE — The smallest **particle** of an **element** or **compound**.

NATURAL SELECTION — The process of **evolution** where life forms that are best adapted to their environment survive, while others don't.

NEUROSCIENCE — The study of the nervous system — especially the brain.

NOBEL PRIZE — A set of awards, established in 1895, given out every year for outstanding achievements in areas including literature, peace, medicine, **physics** and **chemistry**.

NUCLEAR PHYSICS — The study of **subatomic** particles.

NUCLEAR REACTOR — A machine that splits **atoms** and uses the resulting energy to produce electricity.

NUCLEUS — The central part of an **atom** or the part in **cells** that contains **DNA** and controls what the cell does.

PALEONTOLOGY — The study of **fossils** and things that lived in the distant past.

PARTICLE — An extremely small piece of matter.

PASTEURIZATION — A heating process used to kill harmful **bacteria** in some food and drinks.

PHYSICS — The study of how the **Universe** works.

POSITRON — A **subatomic antimatter particle** the opposite of an **electron**.

PREHISTORIC — From a period of time before written history.

QUANTUM PHYSICS — The study of how all **particles** that make up the **Universe** behave at the smallest level.

QUARK — A type of **particle.** Quarks are the building blocks of other particles, including **mesons**.

RADIATION — **Particles** of energy, such as light and heat, given off by a substance.

RADIOACTIVE — When the **atoms** of a substance break down and give off particles of **radiation**.

SEMICONDUCTOR — A material that conducts electricity under certain conditions, but not as well as metals.

SOLAR SYSTEM, THE — The planets, moons and other objects that orbit the Sun.

SPACETIME — The joining of the three dimensions of space (height, width and depth) with a fourth, time.

SPECIES — A group of living things that can breed together.

SUBATOMIC — Smaller than an **atom**, or relating to **particles** smaller than an atom.

SUNSPOT — A darker patch on the Sun's surface that affects the Earth's **magnetic fields**.

UNIVERSE, THE — Everything that exists in time and space.

VACCINE — A substance that makes a patient immune to a disease.

VEIN — A small blood vessel that carries blood to the heart.

WORLD WIDE WEB — A vast network of websites that can be accessed through the **internet**.

X-RAY — A type of **radiation** that can pass through some materials but not others. Used to make photographs of the inside of the human body.

INDEX